AM I OKAY, GOD?

DEVOTIONALS FROM THE SEVENTH DIMENSION

SEVENTH DIMENSION

LORILYN ROBERTS

Am I Okay, God? Devotionals From the Seventh Dimension

Copyright © 2023 by Lorilyn Roberts

4 ed.

Rear Guard Publishing, Inc.

Gainesville, FL 32606

Cover photograph and interior photographs copyright © Shutterstock.com

Standard licensing agreement

Enhanced cover design by Lisa Hainline

Edited by Katherine Harms and Lisa Lickel

All rights reserved. No part of this book may be reproduced or utilized in any form or by any means, electronic or mechanical, or by any information storage and retrieval system—except for brief quotations for the purpose of reviews, without written permission from the publisher.

Scripture taken from the NEW AMERICAN STANDARD BIBLE, Copyright ©

1960, 1962, 1963, 1968, 1971, 1972, 1973, 1975, 1995 by the Lockman Foundation. Used by permission.

Library of Congress Control Number: 2013919095

ISBN: 9780989142656 (k-ebook)

ISBN: 9780989142656 (s-ebook)

ISBN: 9780989142663 (kdp)

ISBN: 9780996532266 (is)

Manufactured in the United States of America

DEDICATION

TO PAULA

my soul sister

FOREWORD

Am I Okay, God? Devotionals from the Seventh Dimension is a companion book to *Seventh Dimension – The Door, a Young Adult Christian Fantasy*. You do not need to have read *The Door* to enjoy these devotionals.

Am I Okay, God? loosely follows Shale's journey to the Seventh Dimension. I hope when you finish this book you will have a better understanding of what it means to be a daughter or son of the king.

CHAPTER 1

AM I OKAY, GOD?

BUT IN ALL these things we overwhelmingly conquer through him who loved us. For I am convinced that neither death, nor life, nor angels, nor principalities, nor things present, nor things to come, nor powers nor height, nor depth, nor any other created thing, will be able to separate us from the love of God, which is in Jesus Christ our Lord.

—Romans 8:37-39

Have you ever asked, am I okay? If so, you aren't alone. I have asked myself that question many times.

Memories still haunt me of bullying by others who accused me of many things. When I was young, I struggled not to believe the lies even when I knew they weren't true. I blamed myself—the only way I knew how to make sense of the accusations.

From *Seventh Dimension – The Door, a Young Adult Christian Fantasy.*

Were there underlings roaming the earth looking for an unfortunate victim? Captivated by the king's eyes, the anguished soul stood still for the first time in front of the fishermen.

From off the lake, a breeze stirred, slowly at first and then gaining momentum. Like onionskin, vaporous creatures peeled from the brain of the madman, and the swirling wind tore at the naked and exposed shape shifters. The black, formless creatures were like bats without bodies.

The dark beings smelled rancid, and the awful odor settled over everything. The demons cowered submissively before the king. The creatures hissed, screeched, and made themselves fools. The fearful pig herders withdrew a safe distance.

"What is your name?" the king asked.

"My name is Legion," one of the demons replied, "for we are many."

The king's power and authority over the spirits was omnipotent. The underlings knew him. They knew the king. The muscles in my shoulders tensed, and my legs twitched. Much-Afraid hid her face under my arm.

The demons begged. "Please, do not send us out of the area." They pointed to the pigs. "Send us among the pigs. Allow us to go into them."

At the king's command, they fled from the man and entered the herd. Their formless bodies slid inside the pigs. I shuddered. The pigs shook violently. The herd, numbering in the thousands, stampeded down the steep bank and headed straight into the lake.

The herdsmen watched their valuable livestock disappear, and they shouted accusations at the king. "By whose authority did you drown our herd?"

They flailed their arms at the anglers, and the shepherds traipsed back up the field resolute for answers. "Who is this man that sends pigs into the lake? By what authority does he do such things?" They continued to argue among themselves.

At first, Cherios, Lowly, Much-Afraid and I were too stunned to speak. Cherios spoke first. "Lowly, that is the king, the king of the garden. He's here. The king is here among us."

—Shale Snyder; Cherios, the rabbit; Lowly, the pig; and Much-Afraid, the dog; chapter twenty-two

---

AS A TEENAGER and even into early adulthood, I believed everyone was more athletic, talented, and smarter than me. Had I missed the blessings that my friends had received? I wasn't able to see my value or worth.

There's a difference, however, between feeling flawed and being a sinner. The Bible tells us that Jesus Christ, the king in *Seventh Dimension – The Door,* did not come to condemn the world, but to save it.

I grew up in a non-Christian home and did not know Jesus Christ. My first introduction to him was in the 1961 Hollywood movie *King of Kings*. I was drawn to Jesus for one reason: his love for the people with whom he came into contact.

I did not feel loved for many years. I think we all suffer from feelings of worthlessness and lack of validation. We live in a fallen world where no one loves perfectly except Jesus Christ. And even though he was perfect and sinless, many still rejected him.

If people can reject the Son of God, who was sinless, how much more can we feel rejected by others who are imperfect?

While it's true you're a sinner, that doesn't make you a bad person. It means you need a Savior. You're created in the image of God and that makes you more than okay. You're wonderfully made. You were bought with a price—Jesus Christ died for you.

You're loved more than you will ever know. God loves you more than your parents, your boyfriend, your girlfriend, your brother, your sister, your spouse—even your dog.

You cannot do or say anything that will make God love you more. You cannot do or say anything that will make God love you less. His nature is unchanging. God is the same yesterday, today, and tomorrow.

I hope to show you in this short devotional book, *Am I Okay, God? Devotionals from the Seventh Dimension,* you're more than okay. You're loved by a perfect God.

When Adam and Eve disobeyed God, sin separated them from their heavenly father. Sin entered the world. Until then, perfection was all Adam and Eve had known, including perfect communion with God in the garden. The first sin created a chasm between God and man. Decay began and has continued to this day.

God banished Adam and Eve from the garden. The price for their disobedience and for everyone born after them was eternal punishment.

Ever since the first sin in the garden, Satan has accused and tormented God's people. The condemnation you feel does not come from God.

In the above excerpt, Jesus performed an exorcism on the demon-possessed man. The naked demons entered the pigs looking for a "home" to possess. Jesus then drowned the pigs and the demons in the lake. The demons had tormented the man relentlessly for years—until Jesus set the man free.

THANK YOU, Jesus, that you have given me life. Let nothing separate me from your love. Let this day be the first day of the rest of my life—the day I receive your unconditional love and no longer believe the untrue things people say.

CHAPTER 2

DARK SECRETS

Would not God have discovered it since he knows the secret of the heart?

—Psalm 44:21

Do you have a secret hidden in your heart—something that is so horrid you wouldn't share it with anyone?

From *Seventh Dimension – The Door, a Young Adult Christian Fantasy.*

"I hid in the closet underneath the stairs—my safe house. Nobody would find me in here."

—Shale Snyder, chapter one

God knows everything about you. Every thought and every deed you've ever done or will do is not hidden from his watchful eyes.

Including secrets. Satan will use anything he can to prevent you from experiencing God's grace. Secrets are among his favorite weapons. The devil derives great pleasure using blackmail. You will never win playing his game. All he has to do is threaten to expose your secret sin—pornography, abortion, cheating, thievery—you name it.

My worst fears from the time I was young involved secret sins. I would convince myself if anyone knew "this or that" about me, I would be on the front page of the *New York Times*.

Seriously, in the past, when I was plagued with guilt, I would lie in bed at night and ponder what would happen if someone told something about me that was slanderous. Many poor souls have committed suicide to escape the judgment of others. Secrets of the heart can imprison you in a living hell. Is that how you want to live your life?

God doesn't want you to live in fear. Bring your hidden sin to your heavenly father, confess it, and receive God's unconditional forgiveness. Remember: God died on the cross to heal you from all your sins—past, present, and future.

Thank you, Jesus, that I no longer want to hide in a closet—or behind a façade. I will seek you in the morning, noon, and night so you can set me free from secret sins.

CHAPTER 3

THE DOOR

"Behold, I stand at the door and knock; if anyone hears my voice and opens the door, I will come in to him and will dine with him, and he with me."

Revelation 3:20

Is God standing at the door of your heart? If he is, it's because he wants to come in and be your friend. He brings heavenly food that has eternal value, food that will feed you spiritually. God knows your needs before you even ask.

FROM *SEVENTH DIMENSION – The Door, a Young Adult Christian Fantasy.*

The door creaked as I turned the handle. I held my breath and peered through the tiny slit. Moving shadows darkened the room.

—Shale Snyder, chapter one

SOMETIMES DOORS ARE CLOSED and padlocked. Experiences from our past haunt us, making us afraid to open them. We want to be healed, but our sorrow and fear may prevent us from taking that leap of faith. We must all face our worst nightmare, but God promises even if we walk through the valley of the shadow of death, he will be there.

Shale was hiding in a closet, afraid of people, haunted by her past and afraid of her future. She was a prisoner of her foolish mistakes and insecurities.

Allow God in—open the door of your heart to the one and only one who can heal you.

THANK YOU, Jesus, for standing at the door and waiting for me to open it. Thank you that you know all my failures and mistakes and don't hold them against me.

I invite you into the secret places that no one else can see. Help me to accept your love and receive your forgiveness. Thank you that you're trustworthy and true, a father and a friend—my Savior.

First, determine if the feelings are from God. Ask God, did I commit an offense against you or another person? Ask God to forgive you and/or help you to go to the person you offended and seek forgiveness.

In Shale's case, she did something wrong. While she made a partial confession to Rachel, she never apologized to Judd.

The guilt grew and became like a cancer, allowing hate to fester until God miraculously healed her—when she confessed.

But suppose you are stricken with false guilt? Someone or something is making you feel guilty when you shouldn't feel that way.

Guilt can draw you towards a loving God or drive you away. How does guilt affect you? If it's making you feel distant, go to God.

Sometimes our pain is so great we can't get past it without counseling. Find someone you can trust and talk to him or her. Have someone pray with you. God never intended for you to walk the Christian life alone. You have a whole body of believers who are the discerning eyes, the patient ears, the loving arms, and the caring souls who want to help you.

Remember, you have an enemy who wants to destroy. He is real and powerful, but God is more powerful than he is. Allow Jesus to take control of your life. Don't give the devil a foothold, lest the small foothold on the side of the mountain becomes the whole mountain. Allow God to set you free from guilt. No sin is so great that God can't heal you from its effects—and even use your story of redemption to glorify him.

Only you, God, can set me free from guilt. Please help me to accept your freedom, and to let go of those things that are not from you.

Help me to let go of false guilt and be set free to accept your forgiveness. Help me to be renewed and filled with your perfect peace.

CHAPTER 5

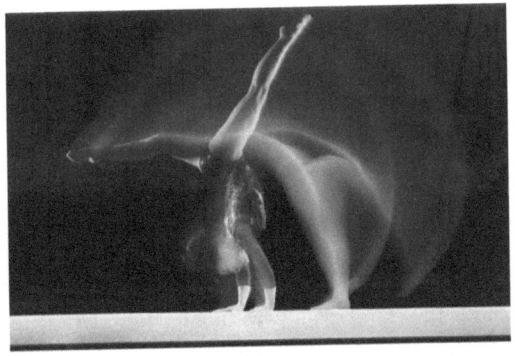

WHAT ABOUT ME, GOD?

When Peter saw him, he asked, "Lord, what about him?"

—*John 21:21*

You're unique. If you were the only person God created, he would have sent Jesus to die for you. God has given you many talents. These gifts were not given to make you great or famous. They were given to you for one purpose: to glorify God.

From *Seventh Dimension – The Door, a Young Adult Christian Fantasy*.

Why would the king want to heal him? My life hadn't changed. What about me? A voice spoke to me, "Don't let others steal your joy. Don't be jealous of others or concerned about not receiving their blessing. Think about the good things the king has given you."

—Shale Snyder, chapter thirty-two

Instead of comparing yourself to others, thank God for the blessings he has given you. Envy is considered one of the seven deadly sins. A person consumed with jealousy is angry and dangerous. Covetousness kills—more than once I have captioned the news where a person was murdered by a maniacal person filled with rage, often fueled by jealousy.

Someday all the material possessions we claim we can't live without will come to an end. Hollywood stars decked out in glittery jewelry will be long forgotten. So will worldly fame and fortune. Heaven has no need of those things. In fact, gold is so "worthless" that the streets of heaven are paved in it.

Will you be there? Remember: God doesn't create junk—he creates beauty—despite the sin that so easily entangles. That's why we need to be redeemed.

Do you know who you are in Christ? Have you forgotten something God did for you? Have you taken your eyes off of the king of kings?

As long as you have a beating heart, you have time to change direction. Don't delay. Today 150,000 people will die. You only have this moment, this second. Act now.

HELP ME, God, to listen to that voice inside of me—to allow your joy to touch my soul and melt my hardened heart. Help me to see your face and let go of all that holds me back. Help me to know you more and more.

Thank you, Jesus, for giving me second chances and third chances and seventy times seventy chances. Thank you for never giving up on me—as your daughter, your son, your child.

http://bit.ly/Video_Am_I_Okay

CHAPTER 6

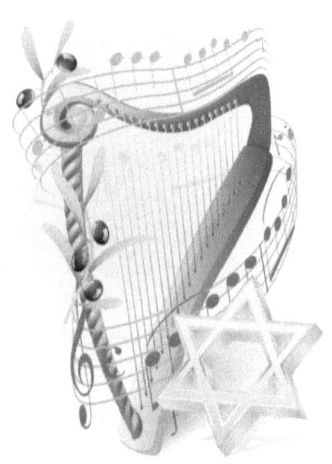

DESIRES OF THE HEART

D<small>ELIGHT</small> <small>YOURSELF</small> <small>IN</small> <small>THE</small> L<small>ORD</small>; and he will give you the desires of the heart.

—*Psalm 37:4*

Have you ever wanted something and thought it would never happen, but then it did happen? God puts longings in our hearts so he can fulfill them.

FROM *SEVENTH DIMENSION – The Door, a Young Adult Christian Fantasy.*

"Can you read that stuff?"

"Sure," Rachel laughed. "But I don't know what it means. You could too if I taught you." Rachel flipped to the first page. "You start on this side." Her finger pointed to a line of Hebrew, and she ran her finger across the page from right to left.

"Really?"

"Yes." Rachel giggled. "So who reads backwards, the English or the Jews?"

"I'd say the Jews. I can say that since I'm not Jewish, right?"

"Why not?"

"Writing would sure be easier if English were right to left. I wouldn't smear my words."

Rachel nodded. "I forget you're left-handed. It's crazy, isn't it—like the Brits drive on the left side and we drive on the right."

We walked for a while not saying anything. I glanced at my friend with her striking olive skin, almond brown eyes, and brown hair. "Do you like being Jewish?"

"Yes, I guess. I don't know any different."

"I wish I was Jewish."

"Why?" Rachel asked.

"It would be neat to be able to say I was something."

—Shale Snyder and Rachel Franco, chapter one

※

OFTENTIMES, we're not aware of the depth of our longing until fulfillment. Then we realize, that's what we wanted.

God fulfilled Shale's longing by taking her to the homeland of the Jewish people. She met the king firsthand; not only that, she met a man with whom she fell in love.

When I graduated from high school, my senior class took a seven-day cruise to the Bahamas, Puerto Rico, and the Virgin Islands. On the last night, the band played into the wee hours of the morning, like the band did on the *Titanic* the night it sank into the Atlantic. When the party began to wind down, the musicians started playing Jewish music. The tourists who weren't Jewish cleared out and congregated around the edges of the dance floor to watch the Jews sing and dance.

What would it be like to be Jewish? I found it astounding that Jews from the entire world shared so much in common through their culture—their music, their dance, and their language.

The Jewish people have survived thousands of years of persecution in many countries and near annihilation in World War II. Yet they still make a joyful noise unto the Lord. More than that, my Lord and my Savior, Jesus Christ, was Jewish. I cried in my heart, "I want what they have—I want to be part of something greater than myself. I want to be part of a spiritual family. I want to be Jewish!"

In early grammar school, I attended Margaret Mitchell School in Atlanta, Georgia. My classmates were predominantly Jewish—and wealthy. My Jewish friends faithfully attended Hebrew classes a couple of times each week. I felt spiritually deprived. My family wasn't Christian or Jewish. What did that make me?

I sometimes wonder if I am Jewish and don't know it. Names have been changed through the centuries, so it's possible. Often when I am around Jewish people, my spirit quickens.

That night so long ago, as I watched the Jews celebrate, my eyes were opened to a spiritual and cultural relationship for which I longed.

Twenty-two years later, I had my opportunity. I was finishing my senior year of undergraduate studies and had an opportunity to travel to the Holy Land. While there, I scuba dived in Eilat, but I didn't get to dance.

Then, one day I was sitting in the Jewish Student Center with a University of Florida student who was helping me with my Hebrew language class. Celebratory music wafted through the walls. I soon heard shouts and cheers.

My student friend paused and said, "Every Thursday night, all the Jewish students come here to Beth Hillel to dance."

"Can anyone join them?" I asked

She replied, "I don't see why not."

Guess where I was the next week? I introduced myself, made it clear I wasn't Jewish, but I loved Jewish music. For the next few years, every Thursday night, I danced with my Jewish friends. Only when the rabbi and his talented wife/teacher moved away did my Jewish dancing end.

Sometimes when we want something that's worthy of God's love, he gives us more than we ask because he is a God of love.

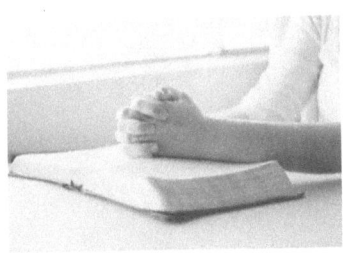

THANK YOU, Jesus, for answered prayers. And those that you don't answer the way I had hoped, thank you that you know what's best for me. Help me to know myself the way you know me. Help me to give you my desires so that you can sanctify them for your glory. Amen.

CHAPTER 7

PRETENDING

THEREFORE, humble yourselves under the mighty hand of God, that he may exalt you at the proper time, casting all your anxiety on him because he cares for you.

—*I Peter 5:6-7*

Has someone done something that upset you and you pretended it didn't happen?

I find it difficult to express my pain when it involves the offense of others. But it is not honest to pretend that I am not bothered by something when I am hurt.

Living in denial about our sin can be just as dangerous. For example, try to convince an alcoholic that he is an alcoholic. Unless he is willing to admit it, he will not be freed from his addiction. If you live in denial, you're limiting your future. You're limiting God's ability to heal you.

How can God help you if you aren't honest—painful are the wounds of the wicked or the dagger of an enemy. Persecution does not live in a pretend world. Satan is for real.

From *Seventh Dimension – The Door, a Young Adult Christian Fantasy*.

Rachel was waiting at the hall lockers. "Shale, why are you standing there? Come on or you'll be late to class."

I walked towards her as the bell rang.

She furrowed her brow. "Are you okay?"

"I'm fine." I smiled, pretending nothing had happened.

"Are you okay?" She furrowed her brow.

"I'm fine." I smiled, pretending nothing had happened."

—Shale Snyder and Rachel Franco, chapter one

JESUS IS KNOWN as the great physician. In the Gospels, Jesus healed many of diseases and afflictions. He not only healed physical ailments but he healed people emotionally, mentally, and spiritually. If someone has done something to you and you can't talk about it, go to the Bible and read the Gospel of Luke, allowing the words from Jesus to soothe your heart.

Jesus went through the shame and humiliation of the cross so you could be set free. Lay your burden at the base of the cross and rejoice that Jesus can carry this burden for you.

There's no greater love than the love of the father for his children. His love is greater than any hurt. You may not believe it because you can exert a lot of energy minimizing an offense.

Cast all your anxiety on the Savior and receive his love. Love covers a multitude of sins.

Denying your pain will only bury it deeper. Minimizing it will not make you feel better. Ask God to help you. His love will lead you to healing, and his word will bring you comfort.

After you have read the Bible and prayed, share your experience with your parent, friend or counselor, trusting God to bring you deliverance.

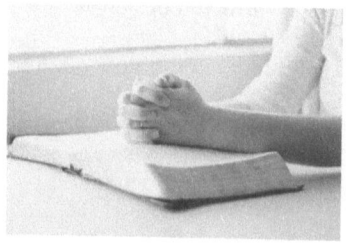

Dear Jesus, thank you for comforting me when I feel down or confused or hurt. Whenever I doubt, I will remember that you love me unconditionally.

Help me to love others the same way you love me.

CHAPTER 8

THE CURSE OF BULLYING

DO NOT GRIEVE the Holy Spirit of God, by whom you were sealed for the day of redemption.

—*Ephesians 4:30*

Has someone taunted you or bullied you?

From *Seventh Dimension – The Door, a Young Adult Christian Fantasy.*

"Why are you praying?" Judd snapped. "We aren't here to pray."

"Accidents happen."

"She should be cursed," Judd exploded.

"Don't say that," Rachel said.

"How do you know it was an accident?" Chumana asked.

I looked away. I couldn't listen. My whole body shook—what kind of curse?

—Shale Snyder, chapter one

THE BEST WAY TO overcome the sting of bullying is to remember how much God loves you. He loves you so much he sent his son, Jesus Christ, to die on a tree 2,000 years ago. Jesus gave his life so that you could have eternal life in him. There's nothing that can take God's gift from you. If you have given your heart to Jesus, God will protect you from the worst spiritual attacks possible. The Holy Spirit seals you and marks you as a follower—you can never lose your salvation.

Again, once you have accepted Jesus Christ into your heart, you're saved. God is not whimsical. He doesn't vacillate like the waves of the sea or give up on you in favor of someone else. Once you accept Jesus Christ into your heart, your ticket to heaven is good. Jesus paid the price.

You can grieve the Holy Spirit by the way you live or by the poor choices you make, but there's nothing—no curse, no bully, or hateful person—that can separate you from Jesus Christ. Jesus sits at the right hand of God interceding on your behalf.

We live in a fallen world. When someone does something unbecoming or questionable, pray for that person. Pray for God's love to touch that soul. Hurt people hurt people.

Don't believe Satan's lies—you can't be cursed. The only control others have over you is the power you give them. No one can force you to think or act a certain way. Remember, you have the Holy Spirit within you.

...GREATER IS *he that is within you, than he that is in the world.*

—*I John 4:4*

We have a taste of heaven here but the best is yet to come. Let God deal with those who bully, but make them accountable for their actions.

Go to a responsible adult. And again, don't believe for an instant someone can curse you.

Thank you that I am created in God's image. Thank you for the protection of the Holy Spirit No curse can befall me because your spirit dwells within me. Thank you that you reside in the most important place in my heart.

http://bit.ly/You_Tube_Book_Trailer

CHAPTER 9

REJECTED AND ALONE

. . .

Therefore, those also who suffer according to the will of God shall entrust their souls to a faithful Creator in doing what is right.

—I Peter 4:19

Never will I [God] leave you or forsake you.

—Hebrews 13:5

Can you talk to your parents about your feelings—your desires, your hurts, your aspirations, and your fears? Perhaps you're afraid they won't understand you. I never felt understood and easily got my feelings hurt. I later learned that sensitivity helped me to be a caring person.

From Seventh Dimension – The Door, a Young Adult Christian Fantasy.

"I couldn't even tell my mother. My father—he left me long ago."

—Shale Snyder, chapter two

🙢

FEAR OF REJECTION RUNS DEEP. We've all felt the sting. I married when I was young and put my husband through medical school. Seven years into our marriage, he had an affair. He divorced me to marry his pregnant girlfriend, much like my father's desertion of me when I was a young girl. Rejection's twin brothers are worthlessness and hopelessness.

Rejection is so familiar to me that I go to great lengths to avoid it. "Am I okay?" I often asked a counselor. I believed if people knew the real me, they would reject me.

I have probably robbed myself of opportunities to further my career or be encouraged in my faith. I still struggle in this area. I am a work in progress.

Rejection comes in many forms. Perhaps you fear you will say the wrong thing at a party.

Rejection may go deeper—a boyfriend drops you, you receive a pink slip at work, or a school you wanted to attend turns down your application.

Ask God to help you sort through your rejected feelings. Read the Bible. Seek out a teacher, a counselor, a coworker, or a fellow student in whom you can confide. If you need help, do not feel ashamed or embarrassed to ask for it.

If you have made poor choices in friends, it's not too late to cut off those relationships. If someone is abusing you physically or emotionally, seek guidance. Don't be afraid, even if someone has threatened you.

If you're pregnant and unmarried, don't abort. Help is available. You will live with that decision for the rest of your life. Don't believe what the world tells you. Abortion kills a beating heart. Call this number: 1-800-366-7773 or go to http://prolifeacrossamerica.org/need-help/.

If you're suffering from the effects of an abortion, don't suffer in silence. There's nothing so awful that God can't handle it. Take that first step—seek help. God will not abandon you. You're not alone.

Not everyone will disappoint you. Not every person is a bully, although it may seem like it at times. People who care about you will help you. Whatever is keeping you awake at night or making you overeat is important. God never meant for his followers to live alone or feel isolated from others.

God never gives up on you, but you must get to the point of recognizing your need and asking for God's help. He can fill in the holes left by those who let you down.

Whenever I feel rejected, I remember how much I am loved by my heavenly father. I will lie on my bed and read the Psalms, remembering God's care is greater than all the wrongs others have done. We have an awesome God who someday will make everything right—all the bad things done to us will no longer be remembered.

God understands how you feel. Jesus was rejected by his own people. The Jewish leaders mocked him and turned him over to the Roman authorities to be crucified. Jesus died willingly for you and for me.

THANK YOU, Jesus, for never leaving me. I know you will walk with me, even carry me, through the lowest moments in my life.

Help me to make good choices.

Help me to be wise and remember I am not alone. Please bring positive people into my life. The Bible says if I ask, you will answer me. Please help me, Lord, to trust in you.

http://bit.ly/Dating_or_Courting

CHAPTER 10

SEVENTH DIMENSION CONNECTION

. . .

...FOR YOU HAVE BEEN BORN AGAIN NOT of seed which is perishable but imperishable, that is, through the living and enduring word of God.

I Peter 1:23

When we meet the king face-to-face, we either become more like him or we walk away, unwilling to submit to his authority.

Remember when the king cast the demons out of the cemetery man and later drowned them in the lake? I shared this in the first devotional. The story in *The Door* comes from the Bible.

While *The Door* is a fantasy, the events that happened surrounding the king are true. If you accept God's salvation through Jesus Christ, Satan and his demons will not be happy about your new-found faith.

🕊

From *Seventh Dimension – the Door, a Young Adult Christian Fantasy.*

Descending from the heavens were beautiful creatures, too numerous to count, decked out in white. They wore glowing robes of dazzling splendor. As they tended to the man Baruch called a king, I watched, too awed to speak and too stunned to know what to think.

A few minutes later, I regained my senses.

"Now you know what an underling is," Baruch said.

"A coward, a bully, a demon." I shook my head, still stunned. "Baruch, you did see all of that, right? I wasn't imagining it."

"Heehaw. Now you know the king."

—Shale Snyder and Baruch, the donkey, chapter eighteen

W<small>HILE WE CAN'T SEE</small> spiritual beings, the Bible makes it clear they visit us in our homes, at work, and in the car—angels and demons alike. Who have you entertained lately? Angels in disguise? Or did you let down your guard. Satan and his demons know how to trip you up.

In Ephesians 2:2, Satan is referred to as the prince of the air. We don't see him because we have physical bodies designed to inhabit this world. I call the realm that spiritual beings inhabit the seventh dimension.

Scientists agree there are many galaxies besides our own. Less understood is how many dimensions there might be. Paul, the apostle to the Gentiles, referred to being taken up into the third heaven. He didn't know if he was in the body or out, but it changed his perspective of God and the future.

Here is something I want you to think about. If part of you changes in the physical dimension, then it's going to affect the spiritual realm.

Planet Earth is the battleground for spiritual activity. While earthly kings go to war to conquer, demons fight for control or possession of unsuspecting people. The demons follow the will of Satan, and as they did to the demon-possessed man in Gadarene, they torture. Even with the demon-possessed man, however, the demons couldn't prevent the man from seeking Jesus, who cast the demons out and later drowned them in the lake.

The only way to protect yourself from spiritual attack is through the armor of God (prayer and reading the Bible), and the indwelling of the Holy Spirit.

Without going too far into the metaphysical aspect, let's examine it in psychological terms. If you respond in a certain way to someone, he will act one way. If you respond in a different way, his response will be different. That's a tiny way of looking at it.

If you change on the inside because of the Holy Spirit's work in your heart, the change will be perceived by others, even on a subconscious level. Remember Newton's law from your science class? For every action, there's always an equal and opposite reaction.

Your responses to the world around you will be different because you're now different. The Bible says when you become saved, you're "born again." Unless you're born again, you can't enter into a relationship with Jesus Christ.

When Shale returned home, she had undergone a metamorphosis. Her responses to her environment were different, forcing those around her to respond differently.

When I was twelve and accepted Jesus into my heart, I felt different. My father remarked a few weeks later, "You have been acting differently. You seem different."

I wish I had shared the reason why with him. I was afraid he wouldn't understand, but I knew why. The Holy Spirit had made a difference in my life.

It's very difficult to change yourself. Try to change one habit in your life and see how hard it is, but when you have a personal relationship with Jesus Christ, he helps you to change. Sometimes the changes are subtle and at other times they are profound.

Sanctification by the Holy Spirit is a life-long process. God wants you to grow and learn. It's in the process that we learn how to live out our salvation. The change in you will affect the world around you in ways that you aren't even aware.

THANK YOU, Jesus, for giving me a new life in you—that I am born again and alive in you. I am thankful the Holy Spirit is helping me to become more like you.

CHAPTER 11

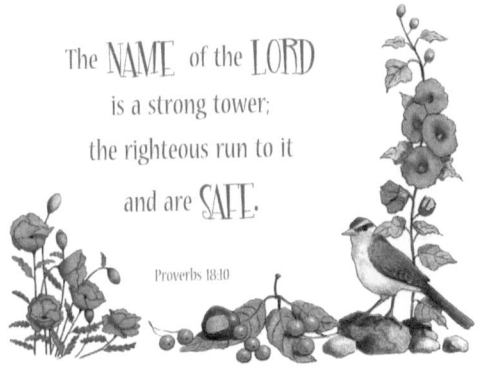

The NAME of the LORD is a strong tower; the righteous run to it and are SAFE.

Proverbs 18:10

BLESSED IS HIS NAME

May his name endure forever; may his name increase as long as the sun shines; and let men bless themselves by him; let all nations call him blessed. Blessed be the Lord God, the God of Israel, who alone works wonders.

—*Psalm 72:17-18*

God has existed since before the beginning of time. He created time. He created the universe. He created you, but he is not a created being.

From *Seventh Dimension – the Door, a Young Adult Christian Fantasy.*

Rachel stood and recited a Jewish prayer. "Blessed is the name of his glorious kingdom forever and ever."

—Rachel Franco, chapter one

In Revelation 1:8, God says, "I am the Alpha and the Omega, who is and who was, and who is to come, the Almighty."

The God of the Bible goes by many names that describe his character. The Jews and the Christians share the same God—

the God of Abraham, Isaac, and Jacob. Christians believe God is three in one—God the Father, God the Son, and God the Holy Spirit. God is not Mohammad, Buddha, or Karma.

God is all powerful and all knowing. Cling to that when life seems out of control, before chaos takes over and leads to frayed nerves, discouragement, and even depression.

God has promised to give you a special name that only he knows when you get to heaven. Think about what name God might give you. Who are you when no one is looking?

God wants to bless you. He knows how to turn hardships into "blessings." These "blessings" will help you to grow in your dependency on him and make you mature.

If everything were easy, you wouldn't need God and you would remain untested. Then when hard times come—and hard times always come—you would fall.

Satan will call you all sorts of names. Don't listen to him. Remember how much God loves you and the name he will someday give you. Honor God above all else and put him first. Experience his presence throughout the day. Read the Bible and pray unceasingly.

THANK YOU, Jesus, that through you I am blessed. If you were all I had, you would be sufficient. There is no one else like you. Thank you for loving me even when I am unlovable.

CHAPTER 12

HOW FAR IS TOO FAR?

NO TEMPTATION HAS OVERTAKEN you but such as is common to man; and God is faithful, who will not allow you to be tempted beyond what you are able, but with the temptation will provide the way of escape also, so that you will be able to endure it.

—*I Corinthians 10:13*

How far is too far when it comes to relationships between young men and women? What does the Bible say about purity?

FROM *SEVENTH DIMENSION – The Door, a Young Adult Christian Fantasy.*

"Word is out about you. I'd hate to see your splattered body sprawled out on the road. It would destroy your father's reputation, cost him his job, and my inheritance—unless Judd gets it first. If I have my way, that won't happen. I need to protect you. From now on, you'll stay where I can see you."

"JUDD GETS WHAT?"

She didn't answer me.

I had no idea what she was talking about. So Judd convinced her I was a tramp even though Daniel had never once been alone with me. Even in the cave, he always insisted the door be open—probably why Judd overheard too much.

—Shale Snyder and Scylla, chapter twenty

In *Seventh Dimension – the Door*, Shale was falsely accused. The fact that she had never been alone with Daniel made her statement she had done nothing wrong more credible.

The most precious gift you can give your future husband or wife on your wedding day is your virginity.

If you are a young lady, make that gift even more special by not allowing yourself to be touched by a man—not even kissed—before you marry him.

If you are a young man, when you see young ladies at the beach or in the store or at church, guard your heart. Be a gentleman in thought and in deed. Treat young girls as if they were your sisters. Treat older women as if they were your mother or grandmother. They are somebody's sister, or daughter, or niece, or grandmother. They are a daughter of the king—and you are a son of the king. Act like one.

Jesus had the utmost respect for women in a society that gave few rights to women. Even the woman caught in adultery, Jesus did not condemn. He sent her accusers away and told her to sin no more (Matthew 12:31)

Young men, if you want a Christian wife, you need to be a Christian man to attract that kind of young lady. The woman you marry will be the mother to your children. Set an example before you get married by treating all women, young and old, with respect.

If you didn't grow up in a Christian home, visit some Christian families and eat dinner with them. Pray with them. God's love for his church is beautifully expressed in a marriage between a Christian man who loves his wife and a Christian woman who loves her husband.

This is a high standard, but it can be done. I recently went to a wedding where the bride and groom shared their first kiss on their wedding day. I marveled that a young couple could have that much self-control and remain pure until they married.

I recently told my younger daughter, and I have told her this many times, a simple expression that goes like this: Clothes on, hands off. One night, however, I made a silly mistake and said, "Clothes off, hands on." She gave me a wry smile, catching my mistake before I did. We both laughed, but she knew exactly what I meant.

Society will tell you it's okay to kiss, touch, and do things that are contradictory to the teachings of the Bible. Don't do it. When you become like the world and see love and sex through the eyes of Hollywood movies, tabloids, and gossip magazines, you're cheapened. You have bought into Satan's lies that these perversions will make you happy. They won't.

You cheat yourself out of what God meant for good between a couple after they become one through marriage. Besides, do you really want those images in your mind on your honeymoon?

If you are a young lady, how would you like your new husband to think about other women he has intimately known when he has just wed you? If you are a young man, do you want to marry a young lady who has cheapened herself with other men?

It's very difficult to keep yourself clean in a world that is inundated with sex and skin and beauty. I recently went on Twitter to find some categories for hashtags for my book. I looked up a common, everyday word and was presented with pornographic pictures of young girls. I was stunned.

If you're normal, you will find these temptations difficult to resist. You're curious, you have hormones, and you're human. But every time you give in to these temptations, the lust of the flesh, you're cheapening your view of something beautiful. God made sex sacred to be shared between a husband and a wife.

Your preoccupation before marriage with lustful thoughts will affect your relationship with the opposite sex. Raw images from the web or pictures from magazines will become imprinted in your mind. You will remember them at inappropriate times. The best way to avoid the temptation is not to allow yourself to be tempted. The Bible says in I Timothy 6:11, "But flee from these things, you man of God, and pursue righteousness, godliness, faith, love, perseverance and gentleness."

Daniel showed great respect for Shale. By opening the door so as not to be alone with her, Daniel respected her. He did not want to put himself into a compromising position with her, that there could ever be rumors spread about their relationship.

Someday you will probably meet a young man if you're a young lady, or if you're a young man, you'll meet a girl to whom you're attracted. If that significant other tells you things like, "If you love me, you will do this," or some other ridiculous statement, have the guts to say "No." Believe in yourself, your value, and your self-worth.

Let me tell you something else. You might be tempted because you want it. Sexual sin doesn't feel bad, it doesn't look horrid, and Satan won't show up with pointed ears and a pitchfork and lounge beside you on the sofa with your date. Unless you have blue blood, you will enjoy romantic relationships. That is normal. Wanting to engage in sexual activity is not what gets you into trouble. Compromising is.

What greater gift can you give your future husband or wife than to be able to tell him or her that you have never shared yourself with anyone else? You have not kissed, you have not fondled, you have not slept, and you have not revealed your unclothed body to someone you have previously dated. Once you have given away that first kiss, you can't get it back. Once a man has touched you, you have given away that part of your body. And once you have been intimate, you're no longer a virgin.

I advise young men and women when they are dating not to even kiss. Once the juices start flowing, it's difficult to turn off the passion. Avoid the situation in the first place.

What Hollywood presents is a sordid picture of reality. I cringe when I see those glamorous pictures of movie stars plastered on the covers of gossip magazines and newspapers —in my heart, I believe them to be the most miserable people on the planet.

Perhaps the saddest tale is that of Lindsay Lohan. What a beautiful, young, talented girl she was in the Disney movie *The Parent Trap* released in 1998. I wondered how long it would be before she posed for a girlie magazine. She is the epitome of someone who had so much to gain and so much to lose. With great talent comes great responsibility and temptation to misuse it. What a waste.

On the other hand, I look at a young man, Tim Tebow, who has used his fame as a way to share his faith. I have watched him from the sidelines for many years because I live in Gainesville, Florida. He was the star quarterback for the Gators, a Heisman Trophy winner in 2007, and took the University of Florida football team to the national championship. He was drafted into the NFL and played a couple of seasons for the Denver Broncos and then a year for the New York Jets before being released on waivers. He was on his way to becoming a distant memory until he was picked up by the New England Patriots. Before the football season started, he was released again. What will people remember him for?

With great faith and opportunity to share in the public arena comes great controversy. People have hated Tebow for no reason except that he is a Christian. Others have looked for opportunities to destroy him. I doubt that history will paint him as a spectacular football player, but there's no doubt in my mind he will take the accolades of his Lord and Savior in heaven over any applause at a football stadium full of cheering crowds and sports pundits.

Any six-foot-four athlete who openly admits he is a virgin and touches the lives of cancer-stricken children in the hospital is a hero. He financially supports a foundation to help orphans in the Philippines where his family once served as missionaries.

I have no idea what else he does, but I know he is not filling the pages of those gossip magazines with unseemly stories. If he were living that kind of life, the whole world would know. Tim Tebow's road has not been easy. He has been scoffed and ridiculed, but through it all, as of this writing, he has walked the straight and narrow path of his convictions.

My point is this: You can do it. You can be like Tim Tebow or you can be like Lindsay Lohan, or somewhere in between. Be careful, however, about the "somewhere in between." God doesn't have good things to say about lukewarm people. In Revelation 3:16, Jesus said, "So because you are lukewarm, and neither hot nor cold, I will spit you out of my mouth."

You must be sold-out to Jesus Christ. You will not have the strength and endurance to overcome the temptations that your sinful nature will crave if you don't. Satan and his demons are relentless. You can't win this battle without becoming a follower of Jesus Christ. Being a fan of his is not sufficient. You will lose every time. My mother used to say, "The road to hell is paved with good intentions." Good intentions aren't good enough. You need the power of the Holy Spirit to win the battle of sex and purity.

If you have messed up in this area, there's healing. There is forgiveness, redemption, and restoration; but there's also pain that comes with all of that work to fix things.

Fortunately, God is in the business of healing broken lives and offers forgiveness. But he doesn't always remove the consequences of your poor choices. If you get a venereal disease, you will suffer. Herpes is ugly. Aids kills. What about if you get pregnant?

Do you want to put yourself in that situation? Do you want to have to explain to your future husband or wife about your sins from the past?

I find relief knowing God will always provide a way to escape temptation. Do everything you can to flee from evil. Don't go to questionable Internet sites. Don't tempt yourself. Don't put yourself into a situation that you might regret later.

Now flee from youthful lusts and pursue righteousness, faith, love and peace, with those who call on the Lord from a pure heart.

–II Timothy 2:22

You belong to God. Keep yourself pure for your future husband or wife, and, above all, for yourself. Stolen fruit may taste good for a moment, but later, it leaves a sour taste in your mouth. Someone once said to me, "A moment of pleasure is not worth a lifetime of regret." That person should have heeded his own advice. It was my ex-husband who told me that before he got his girlfriend pregnant—seven years into our marriage. His foolish mistake shattered me and destroyed our marriage.

Sexual sin affects others—often tragically. Walk away—actually, flee. Ask, what would Jesus want me to do in this situation? And then just do it.

Thank you, Jesus, that you made me the way I am. Help me to remember I am created in your image. Help me to remain pure and save myself for my future husband or wife. Help me to flee from temptation.

My ability to remain pure is impossible without you. I am weak in the flesh but strong in the spirit. Restore the joy of my salvation so that my joy comes from you and not from places where I should not go.

I will remember that my love for you is greater than my love for the world and all that it offers.

Help me to keep my eyes on you. Thank you that you alone are sufficient to flee from immorality in all situations.

http://bit.ly/Piper_On_Sexual_Sin

CHAPTER 13

THE FATHER OF LIES

. . .

Jesus said [to some Jewish unbelievers]: "You are of your father the devil, and you want to do the desires of your father. He was a murderer from the beginning, and does not stand in the truth, because there is no truth in him. Whenever he speaks a lie, he speaks from his own nature, for he is a liar and the father of liars."

—John 8:44

Despite your blemishes, you're a child of the king. But your beauty shouldn't come only from your outward appearance but from your inward radiance.

From *Seventh Dimension – The Door, a Young Adult Christian Fantasy.*

"I'll make you a beautiful princess," he [the serpent] promised.

The desire to be talented and sought after by handsome young men consumed me.

—Shale Snyder, chapter twenty-six

THE TRUTH IS, those provocative pictures of men and women on the cover of *Vogue* and other magazines have been edited with Photoshop to make the models look beautiful. Give me a photograph of yourself and I can make you as glamorous as you want to be.

A professional book designer manipulated the cover of *Seventh Dimension–The Door* in Photoshop. The girl had no blouse on—we added that. Her long hair dipped into the water so we cut it. I didn't want a mermaid. We sprinkled golden glitter on the surface of the water and added a waterfall to the background. We enhanced the bird and added highlights behind the girl to do one thing—to draw your attention to Shale Snyder, the main character in *Seventh Dimension – The Door*.

We can do that because we can manipulate what the eye sees. But what about what is underneath the skin or that outer layer that we can't see? Shale was tempted to believe the serpent's lie to make her beautiful on the outside. Save for her friend, Daniel, she would have been consumed by the temptation.

She wanted to be beautiful, but what she truly wanted was to feel valued by somebody. Her self-worth and self-esteem had been bruised by others. She was persuaded to believe the lie because she was desperate for love.

Beauty, money, wealth—all those things tempt us into believing that if we had this or that one thing, then everything would be great.

Satan lives in the spiritual realm and when you enter that realm of questioning and seeking answers, you will be confronted with choices. The serpent wants to convince you that he can give you a shortcut to happiness.

If you spend all of your time making yourself beautiful on the outside but don't spend time with God developing your relationship with him on the inside, you will be a trophy—a trophy of the devil.

God wants all of you. Don't be led astray. Find your joy in the Lord, and if you have wandered, come back. Remember your first love.

Young ladies may find this hard to believe, but a man of God will seek the beauty of Jesus in you. A godly man will be drawn to your soul that is enraptured with the Holy Spirit. He will see your love for the king, your compassion toward others, your kindness for animals, and a heavenly beauty that surpasses the outward beauty you think you need to catch a young man.

Besides that, if God wants you to marry, he has the perfect man already picked out for you. You don't need to compromise or do things you might regret later. You don't need to wear dresses up to your hips or low-cut blouses to grab the attention of a handsome suitor.

If you're a young lady, would you want a man who was attracted to you only because of your outward beauty? That kind of beauty fades. Breasts sag, hair turns gray, wrinkles appear, and varicose veins pop out.

If you are a young man, young Christian ladies want a man who "walks the walk" and not just "talks the talk." A real Christian woman can spot a counterfeit Christian man within a few minutes of conversation. A real Christian woman can feel his lustful gaze and she can read his carnal thoughts. In fact, any woman will know when a man is not treating her with respect, even if she doesn't say so.

I tell my daughters, if you want a Christian marriage, find a man who really, really, really loves the Lord, and then he will love you.

Sadly, in today's world, there aren't enough young truly committed Christian men. Part of it is probably due to our Western culture, where young men have bought into the idea that it's okay for them to sow their wild oats before getting married. Beware, though, some of those wild oats contain poison.

In Hollywood, you're given a star people walk on that symbolizes greatness. Is that what you want? In heaven, you will be given a crown, or even many crowns, depending on how you've lived your life. Would you rather have a star on the Hollywood Walk of Fame that might be destroyed in an earthquake or a crown of righteousness that will never fade? In fact, there are many kinds of crowns to be awarded to the saints for their faithful deeds.

Here are some Bible passages that describe the kinds of crowns that await the believers when they arrive in heaven.

[II Timothy 4:8] The crown of righteousness, given to those who long for the Messiah's return.

[I Corinthians 9:25-27] The incorruptible crown, given to those who have exercised self-discipline and self-control over their bodies and thoughts.

[James 1:12] The crown of life, given to those who have endured patiently through trials.

[I Peter 5:4] The crown of glory, given to pastors and others who have faithfully served God.

[I Thessalonians 2:19] The soul winner's crown, given to those who have brought many followers into the kingdom.

The temptation to buy into Satan's lies is great, but God's love is greater. Remember your Lord and Savior at those moments when you are tempted, "…and the things of this world will grow strangely dim in the light of his mercy and grace." [lyrics to *Turn Your Eyes Upon Jesus*].

Young men and young ladies, adorn yourself with thoughts that will captivate your soul. Thoughts of beauty when you embrace God's creation. Thoughts of wonder at the testimony of those who have suffered because they love Jesus.

Look for good in the world because it's there. It won't be found in tabloids or on store aisles stocked with overpriced items promising fame, beauty, or fortune. God's insurmountable beauty will be found in sunsets, in family relationships, in friendships that honor God, in Thanksgiving dinners and Bible studies and fellowship with other believers.

A smile on your face can lighten up a room. Acceptance in your eyes can reassure someone who is sad. A hug can make someone feel wanted. A kind word can tear down strongholds that Satan has built—you're beautiful just the way you are.

Young ladies, you don't need to do anything to make handsome men desire you—for the wrong reasons. Love the Lord your God with all your heart mind, and soul. He will send you the right soul mate and husband at his appointed time.

And young men, if you want God's absolute best wife in the world, save yourself for the one he created to be your helpmate. Make women desire you because of your love for God.

THANK YOU, Jesus, for helping me to trust you in my relationships with the opposite sex. Help me to trust you for my future husband or wife.

Please help me to wait. Help me to grow in maturity so I can someday be the wife or husband you call me to be. I want to be content where you have put me, single or married. My hope for a future spouse is found in you.

http://bit.ly/LR_Satan

CHAPTER 14

WHICH ANIMAL AM I MOST LIKE?

BUT NOW ASK THE BEASTS, and let them teach you; and the birds of the heavens, and let them tell you. Or speak to the earth, and let it teach you; and let the fish of the sea declare to you. Who among all these does not know that the hand of the Lord has done this, in whose hand is the life of every living thing, and the breath of all mankind? Does not the ear test words as the palate tastes its food?

—Job 12:7-11

Which animal do you identify with in *Seventh Dimension – The Door*? Do you perceive your nature to be like Worldly Crow; Cherios, the rabbit; Baruch, the donkey; Much Afraid, the dog; Nevaeh, the bird; or Lowly, the pig?

"Will the king always be with me?"

"Always. The seventh dimension is within you. The animals represent parts of your character. Your suffering has produced good fruit. And always remember, the king is your heavenly father."

—Shale Snyder and Astello, chapter thirty-seven

ALL OF US are multifaceted and complex, intricately woven together into extraordinarily complicated human beings. The Creator isn't a novice at creating life. Look around you. He can breathe life into building blocks simply by speaking them into being.

Good and evil are at war against each other in the world and within ourselves. We will never be free of temptation until we enter heaven's gates.

All of us at one point or another have been as wicked as Worldly Crow or as heavenly as Cherios, the rabbit, or Nevaeh—the unusual bird in the garden. Did you know that Nevaeh is "heaven" spelled backwards?

Cherios comes from the word "charity," which means generous actions to aid the poor, ill, or helpless, or to devote one's life to love. Cherios gave her life as she praised the king before the demons in the Hall of Darkness.

The other animals were redeemed by the king. Baruch means blessed. In *The Donkey and the King*, Baruch was a temperamental donkey that struck out on his own and became lost. The king sent the sheep to find him in the wilderness, just as the king searches out each one of us when we become lost.

You may be feeling lost right now. Have you made foolish choices? The good news is that Jesus Christ won't leave you there. Even if you're as wicked as Worldly Crow, God still forgives if you ask for forgiveness. The king is in the business of fixing problems and situations that seem hopeless. The king's way is even better than your way.

Maybe you're like Lowly the pig. Do you feel worthless? God has given you everything you need to become the person he created you to be. Not one cell or gene is missing because

God made a mistake. He's gifted you with what you need to glorify him.

If you want to be a doctor, God has given you the brains and the ability to be one. If you want to be a dancer, God has made you graceful and athletic. If you want to be a teacher, God has given you the ability to teach. Not only that, he has given you the desire to want to do the things he created you to do.

If you enjoy painting, God made you to paint. God needs Christians in all walks of life. We can't all be lawyers or bankers or chefs. Perhaps the job you will have when you graduate from high school, technical school, or college doesn't yet exist. My profession wasn't around twenty-five years ago. The world is constantly changing.

Perhaps you're like Much-Afraid, the dog that pursued Shale. The Bible tells us in I Peter 5:7: "Cast all your anxiety on him because he cares for you."

This is much easier said than done, but just as Much-Afraid stood up to the demon-possessed man in the cemetery, God will give you supernatural power to overcome your worst fears. He does not mean for you to live in fear of the future or regret about the past.

Sometimes things don't turn out the way you want them to, but it's not because God failed or you failed. It's because if you put your trust in Jesus, he knows what's best in every circumstance. Jesus cares about the process more than the outcome.

The only moment you have is right now. We aren't guaranteed tomorrow. And we don't want to look back on our past with regret. The Bible tells us in Ephesians 5:16 that we should make the most of every opportunity.

The devil and his demons won't like it if you read the Bible or pray to God daily. Expect at those moments when you're most like Jesus to be attacked. The Bible says in 1 Peter 5:8 that the enemy prowls around like a roaring lion looking for someone to devour.

You must not give up. Shale was tested and overcame and you can overcome, too. The battle is a spiritual one.

I imagine angels all around with swords in hand knocking down demonic strongholds. We must claim the power of the risen king to overcome demonic influence, the Worldly Crow part of us, and rely on the Holy Spirit.

Jesus Christ is not in the tomb. He is risen. He is sitting at the right hand of God the Father in heaven, interceding for you.

You have a future and a hope. You were made with heavenly hands in your mother's womb. When you start to doubt your value in God's eyes, remember what Nevaeh whispered in Shale's ear, "You're a daughter of the king."

Thank you, Lord, that I am fearfully and wonderfully made—that you knitted me in my mother's womb and knew me even before I was born.

I thank you for tall giraffes and whimsical butterflies and slimy snails and hooting owls. If this world can have so much vitality and variety, as darkened as it is with sin, I can only imagine the perfect world that lies in wait.

Let the animals teach me how to be kind. Help me to listen—to the call of the wild, the purring of a kitten, the roaring of a lion, or the cry of an abandoned dog. Help me to be your heart in a world that needs caring people to speak up for those who can't speak for themselves.

May I grow more like you as I care for the animals I meet. May I be as wise as a serpent and as innocent as a dove. May I remember that a kind person is kind to his animals even when no one is looking.

CHAPTER 15

I AM THE WAY

FINALLY, brethren, whatever is true, whatever is honorable, whatever is right, whatever is pure, whatever is lovely, whatever is of good repute, if there is any excellence and if anything worthy of praise, dwell on these things.

—*Philippians 4:8*

What did Jesus mean when he said, "I am the way, the truth, and the life?"

From *Seventh Dimension – The Door, a Young Adult Christian Fantasy.*

What did I want? If I knew, would I be willing to risk everything to obtain it? I gazed at the lake—where was the king headed? I wished I knew the lake's secrets. If he was the king from the garden, how did he get here? He seemed powerful in some ways but not in others.

—Shale Snyder, chapter twenty-three

Shale faced the same issues that you and I face today—discovering the truth and what it means. How should I live, and is Jesus who he said he was?

Many religions offer you multiple paths to salvation or fulfillment. Baha'i embraces all religions and states that God sent messengers—like Jesus, Buddha, Moses, and Muhammad—to progressively teach us about God's nature.

Islam teaches that if your good works outweigh your bad, and Allah wills it, he will let you enter into paradise.

Hinduism and Buddhism claim you go to heaven after many reincarnations when at last you become one with God.

Some Jews still wait for the Messiah's return. Each year during the Passover Seder, a Jewish custom is to pour a cup of wine, "the cup of Elijah," and send a young child to the door to look for the prophet who is to herald in the coming of the Messiah.

Unitarians believe you can get to heaven any way you want and not to worry about the afterlife.

Wiccans don't believe there's a need for salvation.

What do you think?

In *Seventh Dimension – the Door*, Shale went on a journey—it was her path. No two journeys through life are exactly the same. God knows which path you will take—but his unconditional love gives you free will to choose.

Along the way, you will be exposed to many "truths" and many lies. You must learn to discern truth from falsehood. The Bible says Satan is the "father of lies" (John 8:44). When Jesus stood before Pontius Pilate, shortly before being crucified, Pontius Pilate asked him, "What is truth?" (John 18:38).

Truth stood in front of Pontius Pilate, and yet he did not recognize the truth. Instead, he denied that truth, condemning

Jesus the Messiah to death.

If truth stood before you, would you recognize him? Could you taste his goodness? Could you feel his breath and know it was the breath of life? Could you perceive God's gentle touch? Would your mind be quickened if God called your name?

It's a scary thing to be confronted with the truth of Jesus Christ and yet deny him—deny his power, deny his sacrifice, and deny his love.

Satan makes our life difficult. Our sin nature leads us astray. But if we confess our sins and acknowledge Jesus Christ as the way, the truth, and the life, we won't be fooled into believing untruths. Nothing makes Satan and his demons more angry than hearing the name of Jesus. Fill your heart with God's love, praise his holy name, and they will flee.

Thank you, Jesus, that you are the way, the truth and the life. Help me to be more like you. Help me to be discerning in all things and protect me from being led astray.

Help me to focus on what is true and noble and be an example to others. Let my little light shine before men and light the path to you. Help me to know the way of salvation through living out my faith. In my life, Lord, be glorified.

CHAPTER 16

LIFE IS NOT FAIR

The Lord is my shepherd, I shall not be in want. He makes me lie down in green pastures, he leads me beside quiet waters. He restores my soul. He guides me in paths of righteousness for his name's sake.

Even though I walk through the valley of the shadow of death, I will fear no evil, for you are with me. Your rod and your staff, they comfort me. You prepare a table before me in the presence of my enemies. You anoint my head with oil, my cup overflows.

Surely goodness and love will follow me all the days of my life, and I will dwell in the house of the Lord forever.

Psalm 23

Is life fair? Perhaps your family refers to you as the "black sheep," the one who is different from everyone else.

I believed I was born under a cloud. My birthfather left my mother when I was two and I didn't meet him again until I was thirty. It wasn't until I was six that I realized most of my friends had a father. I couldn't imagine why anyone needed one of those. I remembered when mine left and he never came back. Being raised by a single mother seemed normal to me—until people asked where my father was. I didn't know.

Perhaps you can relate to me. Does life seem fair?

FROM *SEVENTH DIMENSION – the Door, a Young Adult Christian Fantasy (*in this excerpt, Shale has met her birthfather for the first time, and she asks him why he left her):

Why was this so difficult? I needed to know the truth. I'd try again.

"I used to wonder what it would be like if we met. I dreamed of spending time with you. I didn't like growing up without a father. Something was missing. I felt like a doughnut with a big hole in the middle. Mother never understood me—and she sure didn't like you by the time I was old enough to realize everyone else had a father but me."

—Shale Snyder and Brutus Snyder, chapter fifteen

LIFE IS NOT FAIR—IN my opinion, most of the time. Bad things happen. No matter how hard you try, things don't work out the way you think they should.

In my case, as a child, I tried to make sense of why bad things happened. I came to the conclusion that I must be flawed. I believed my parent's divorce was my fault. I thought people didn't like me (and bullied me) because I wasn't likable.

FOR AS HE thinks within himself, so he is.

—*Proverbs 23:7*

MY DAUGHTER WAS the Level 8 Florida Gymnastics Champion for the vault in 2012. In 2013 during the state competition the equipment moved when she placed her hands on the vault. She bailed out of the vault to avoid getting hurt. Because she was so freaked out after her first run, she was unable to do the second vault and bailed out again. She scored a zero on the event which disqualified her from competing at the regional meet. If you have ever competed at a high level in any sports, you know how devastating this was to both of us.

Perhaps you've spent hours preparing a report and just before you save the final draft, your computer crashes and eats it. You have to turn it in tomorrow and now you can't. You're devastated.

Life is not fair, but it's not because you are bad. If you think you're no good, you will treat yourself with disdain. Others will pick up on the subliminal messages you send and may treat you disrespectfully. What should you do, though, when life is not fair? How do you not blame yourself for the bad things that happen?

Shale's life wasn't fair. It wasn't her fault that her father abandoned her. She didn't deserve to be bullied. Her life was a mess—and she knew it deep down. She knew there was something she wanted, something she needed, but she didn't know what it was.

Sometimes bad things happen to good people.

It would be easy for me to cite a few Bible verses and tell you to get on with it, make lemonade out of lemons and quit holding pity parties on Saturday night. After all, there's always someone who is worse off than you. But it would not help you.

Are there things you can do besides feel sorry for yourself?

Try writing down all the things in your life that you're angry about, like Shale told God all the things that made her angry. Better yet, start keeping a diary and jot down your feelings each day.

If you're like me, you might find it difficult to share your innermost thoughts. Shale was unable to express her hurts and that's why Much-Afraid, the dog, was important to her. Shale kept resentments bottled up inside. She had no one who would listen to her, no one to confide in—once Rachel could no longer be her friend. She told God exactly how she felt by keeping a diary.

Maybe you don't hate God but you would like some answers. Sometimes I want answers, too. Why did God allow this or that to happen? Why did my father leave me when I was a child? As wonderful as some adoptive fathers are, melding together as a family can take months or even years.

Have you been honest with yourself and listed several items on your sheet? If not, how can you be honest with God? Believe me, God won't be upset with you if you do this.

Now take your list and go down each item and give it to God. God knows everything on your list before you even tell him. But there's something healing about confessing to God the things that frustrate you and upset you.

This is part of building trust in God—that you can go to him, knowing he will understand you when you tell him how you feel.

God wants to have a relationship with you. God never changes. It's you and me who change. We forget all about God or stay too busy. God is waiting for you to come to him.

. . .

Cast all your anxiety on him because he cares for you.

—I Peter 5:7

That means everything that gets you upset, frustrated, or angry. If it's your family—tell God so. If it's a teacher, tell God so. If it's a coach, tell God so. Confess your heart to the Great Physician who cares.

Things may not change on the outside. Your family may not ever understand your needs, and, quite frankly, they may not even care. But when you go to God and confess how you feel, something changes on the inside. You become a different person—a tiny bit, because you have given all that negative stuff inside of you to God. The Holy Spirit, or the Comforter, will come alongside and encourage you, lift you up, speak to your innermost being, and remind you that you belong to Jesus.

You might go to God today and expect him to change everybody and fix your problems, only to discover later nothing has changed. You soon realize you still have to face your teacher tomorrow or live with your disagreeable family or deal with the rejection of a close friend.

Shale's world didn't change when she was locked up in her room for days at a time, but she found solace in her relationship with the king. Your relationship with Jesus Christ will make a difference.

Get out your Bible, dust it off, and start reading. Read the Psalms, written by David, found in the Old Testament. David was a man after God's own heart and the most famous and best king of Israel. He spent much of his life being treated unfairly by others, but he loved God deeply. Meditate on these words.

Dear God, help me to see others as you see them so I don't blame myself for things that are not my fault. When I'm angry with someone, I will remember you love me. It is that love that will compel me to lay down my rights to get even or to "prove" I am right.

Help me to remember I am responsible for taking care of myself to the extent of my ability. I can listen to music when I am sad, go for a walk in the woods. sing, keep a journal, and spend time with positive people. I can watch a funny movie or read a good book.

I may not be able to change some things. Please help me, God, to accept those things I can't change. Please help me to change the things I can, and the wisdom to know the difference.

Help me to remember I am not responsible for other people's bad choices. I am only responsible for how I choose to react to those choices. Help me to remember I am a child of God and deeply loved by you.

CHAPTER 17

I DON'T WANT TO FORGIVE

THEN PETER CAME and said to him, "Lord, how often shall my brother sin against me and I forgive him? Up to seven times?" Jesus said to him, "I do not say to you, up to seven times, but up to seventy times seven."

—*Matthew 18:21-22*

Everyone agrees forgiveness is something we should do until we are confronted with the unforgiveable.

From *Seventh Dimension – The Door, a Young Adult Christian Fantasy*

I stood frozen as if shot with a stun gun. How could he be here? Memories hijacked me—the curse he put on me two years ago, the attack in the hallway, shaming me with the worm, and all the things too numerous to mention. He had made my life hell. I hated him. How dare he follow me here! I began to hyperventilate, feeling my way behind me with my hands.

"Don't come near me or I'll kill you."

—Shale Snyder and Judd Luster, chapter twelve

Did Shale have the "right" to hate Judd? After all, he had tried to put a curse on her when she was young, physically attacked her in the hallway at school, and bullied her relentlessly.

How about Judd? Was he justified in how he treated Shale? Shale had hurt Judd when she accidentally killed his puppy. Do two wrongs make a right?

I have been a Christian since I was twelve years old. At thirty I rededicated my life to Jesus Christ when I read the book of Romans in the New Testament. My desire to read the Bible was prompted when my husband left me for another woman.

At the core of my struggle was the fact I didn't want to forgive my husband. I wanted to hold on to my pain because it was familiar. I had been in a lot of pain for a long time. I didn't know how I would live without him and I didn't feel like he deserved to be forgiven.

Besides that, I was grieving. Emotionally I was too distraught to be rational about the concept of forgiveness. My sorrow was like a stranglehold, deep and relentless.

Once I realized I needed to forgive, I wasn't sure I could. I'd died a thousand deaths and there was no way I could forgive anyone who had hurt me that badly.

Has someone done something to you and you can't seem to let go? Have you ever done something to someone that caused that person immense pain?

Over the course of time, the raw memories will fade. The pain may ease, but will probably always be there. Despite the hurt, forgiveness brings acceptance and peace.

Hate is one of the strongest emotions of the human psyche. Martin Luther King said, "Darkness cannot drive out darkness; only light can do that. Hate cannot drive out hate; only love can do that."

Shale's hatred toward Judd spilled out into other areas of her life, particularly in her relationship with God. She angrily blamed him for sending her broken toys, taking away her best friend, giving her parents who didn't understand her and teachers who hated her. Most of all, she was angry at God for teasing her with a stray dog she couldn't keep.

When you refuse to forgive, you harbor bitterness. You can't compartmentalize your feelings. Being unable to forgive will eventually take over your entire personality. Have you ever met a vindictive or bitter person?

Thoughts, emotions, and actions will be affected. Just as cancer invades a person's body, hatred knows no boundaries.

Preoccupation with hate can become a full-time job. It takes a lot of energy to stay angry—energy that could be used for more constructive purposes. Satan is the only winner when you refuse to forgive. Is your inability to forgive worth it?

Dear Jesus, I want to forgive, but I don't know how. Help me to let go of my pain. Help me not to hate. Even if I were willing to forgive, it wouldn't change what has already happened, but I don't want to be separated from you. Please help me to forgive.

CHAPTER 18

UNFORGIVENESS HURTS

Be strong in the Lord and in his mighty power. Put on the full armor of God so that you can take your stand against the devil's schemes. God gives us the belt of truth, the breastplate of righteousness, our feet fitted with readiness, and the shield of faith. We have the helmet of salvation and the sword of the Spirit, which is the Word of God.

—Ephesians 6:10-17

If you are unwilling to forgive others, how can you expect God to forgive you?

FROM *SEVENTH DIMENSION – The Door, a Young Adult Christian Fantasy.*

"I HATE YOU, God—you hear me? You send me broken toys and take away my best friend, give me parents that don't understand me and teachers that hate me. That's fine. I can take it. You hear me? Then you tease me with a dog I can't have." The bare walls were silent and I buried my face in my arms and sobbed.

—Shale Snyder, chapter four

THERE IS ONLY one person whom hate completely destroys. The person who hates. Hate is so all-consuming that it drives people to do horrific things they wouldn't normally do.

Hitler hated the Jews, and as a result, over six million Jews were slaughtered during World War II. 1.6 million Russians died when Lenin came to power. How many people died under Stalin's regime? At least 20 million people were killed.

This is hate at its worst. When hateful men are in positions of power, they are capable of inflicting the most horrid and despicable acts on others. Many of those victims were flogged, beaten, raped, maimed, and mutilated for no reason —just because of hate.

You may not have done something as horrid as one of these men, but whenever you hate, you're giving the devil a foothold into your heart. Hate robs you of joy. It steals from you the blessings of God. Remember, the devil wants all of you—including your soul.

Jesus said to Peter, "Satan has asked to sift you as wheat (Luke 22:31)."

These words by Jesus are astonishing. First, they reassure me that Satan has no power except that which God allows him to have. Second, they remind me that the battle I fight is a spiritual one—a battle that I can't win without Jesus coming to my aid. While we are human, Satan is a real spiritual being with immense power. Our only protection from him is to arm ourselves with the spiritual weapons of war.

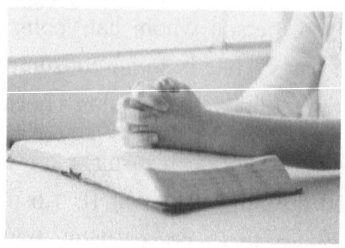

Dear Jesus, even when I don't feel like forgiving, help me to forgive anyway. Even when the world says I have my rights, help me to forgive anyway. Even when I can't forgive in my own strength, help me to forgive anyway. Even when the person whom I have forgiven doesn't recognize the cost, help me to live in forgiveness anyway.

http://bit.ly/Famous_Atheists_Last_Words

CHAPTER 19

THE POWER OF FORGIVENESS

BUT JESUS WAS SAYING, *"Father, forgive them; for they do not know what they are doing." And they cast lots, dividing up his garments among themselves.*

—Luke 23:34

The root cause of hate, I believe, is the lack of forgiveness. We must forgive. If we are unable to forgive, the hateful feelings will destroy us.

Not forgiving separated me from God. How could I feel forgiven by God if I was unwilling to extend that same forgiveness to someone else? Even if I said in my heart, "I forgive my ex-husband," my lack of forgiveness would re-emerge later when something triggered the return of painful memories. I couldn't get forgiveness to stick. I soon realized, I had to commit to the process of forgiveness—a lifestyle, a mindset, a choice. Every time I started to become bitter, I had to go through the process of forgiveness all over again. In my case, forgiveness took me a long, long time.

Without the Holy Spirit's help, I would not have been able to forgive my ex-husband. Fortunately, after a period of time, I realized my love for God was greater than my bitterness and regret over mistakes I had made in the marriage—strong enough to overcome my intense sadness and depression. Through God's love and power, I was at last able to forgive completely.

Our model for forgiveness is Jesus Christ. Jesus forgave us as he hung naked on a cross. We don't deserve his forgiveness or grace. He simply loved us that much. We deserve to die and pay the price for all the mistakes and sins we have committed, but instead, Jesus died and paid the price for us.

There's nothing more powerful than seeing someone who has been hurt exercise his will to forgive. If we choose to hate, the devil will be our master. If we choose to follow the example that Jesus set for us, we will love, and he will be our master. To love in these circumstances is not a feeling. It's a choice.

FROM *SEVENTH DIMENSION – The Door, a Young Adult Christian Fantasy.*

"I'm nothing more than a worm, like that worm lying on the sidewalk that Judd wanted to crush. There's nothing good inside me except that which was put there by the king. Just as I rescued that worm from his tormenter, my king will rescue me, too, and crush your head [the serpent]. The king promised, if you forgive others, your heavenly father will also forgive you. I am forgiven."

—Shale Snyder, chapter thirty-five

MORE FROM *SEVENTH DIMENSION – The Door, a Young Adult Christian Fantasy.*

. . .

Magical stirrings from deep within bubbled forth and overflowed. Freedom beckoned me.

I countered their lies, "He'll always live in my heart. You can't hurt me anymore"...suddenly, the demons began to shrink—smaller and smaller they became, right before my eyes. As the underlings shrunk, they underwent a metamorphosis. They shrank smaller and smaller and we grew larger and larger. Soon the underlings had shape shifted into nothing more than puny snakes. Even though they hissed, their voices became as a little mouse's before a taunting cat.

—Shale Snyder, chapter thirty-five

Forgiveness is never easy. With great forgiveness comes great grace. Great grace is never cheap. Jesus Christ paid the ultimate price to forgive us by shedding his blood on the cross. We can't give him back his life—Christ willingly allowed himself to be crucified so that he could give us eternal life. It was a choice he made. It's a choice we must make—the choice to forgive.

Sometimes it requires a recommitment—as in my case, when I recommitted my life to Jesus Christ. I knew I needed more faith to forgive. I was running on an empty gas tank, and the only way to fill it up was to allow God's Spirit to work in my heart. I had to make a conscious choice to forgive my ex-husband. I had to ask God to help me do it. I couldn't do it on my own. I couldn't conjure up enough goodness within me to do it without his help.

God is gracious and loving. We are forgiven by God, and we must extend that forgiveness to others if we want to be like

Jesus. If forgiveness was cheap, it would not have cost Jesus his life. But our forgiveness couldn't be bought with anything less.

We must lay down our rights, lay down our hurts, and lay down our desires to retaliate. We might have to go back to God and ask for his help many, many times to enable a lifetime of living in forgiveness. And each time we recognize our need for him, he gives us everything we need to abide in him.

Dear Jesus, I lay down my rights at the foot of the cross. I open my hands and release my anger. I forgive.

Be glorified, Lord, for any good thing that comes out of this. I choose to love you, and with your love, I am set free to once again live in peace.

Lorilyn Roberts' testimony

CHAPTER 20

I HATE MY STINKING SIN

Do not let the sun go down while you are angry, and do not give the devil a foothold.

Ephesians 4:26b-27

We will never be free of our sin until we get to heaven. Satan will never give up taunting us, bullying us, and shaming us. As long as we live here he is the "prince of the air."

FROM *SEVENTH DIMENSION – The Door, a Young Adult Christian Fantasy.*

We climbed the stairs to my room and a veil of darkness shrouded me—Fifi's dead body appeared to me in a vision once more at the bottom of the stairs. I had hoped the memory wouldn't torture me anymore, that the king would heal me. Why hadn't me? I grabbed the post to catch my balance. Rain started to fall.

—Shale Snyder, chapter twenty-nine

SATAN PROWLS around like a roaring lion hunting down unsuspecting victims. In I Corinthians 10:13, Paul tells us that

"God is faithful, and he will not let you be tempted beyond what you can bear."

For many years, I hated many things about my life. I even hated myself at times—the fact that my father left me, that I grew up in a broken home, that I failed the first grade, that I had a speech impediment, and that I was clumsy. I felt misunderstood and unappreciated by others. I had no self-worth. I was an outcast in social circles at school. No one liked me except the smart kids, once they figured out I wasn't dumb, and so I hung around with a bunch of nerds.

I preferred to be alone with a good book or playing the guitar. I didn't care about loud parties or drinking or concerts or smoking or any of those things in which teenagers get involved—to their detriment. I was a loner because—well, I liked being alone. My parents thought something was wrong with me.

When I got married, I expected my husband to fix me. After all, he was going to be a doctor and he should be able to be all that I needed—to make up for what I lacked in the past. The truth is, the only thing that could fix me was a personal relationship with Jesus Christ.

The sad part is this: nothing was wrong with me. I wasn't flawed or defective or weird or antisocial or stupid or bad. I actually was and still am very creative, brilliant in some ways, self-sufficient, and uniquely made in God's image. And so are you. I was and still am a sinner. And so are you.

Unconditional love covers a multitude of sins. That kind of acceptance and validation can only come from Jesus Christ. There's no pill, no lover, no vacation, no job, no friend, and no food that can fill that spiritual void and remove the sting of lies and false accusations—only the healing power of our risen Savior.

If you're like Shale, a victim of circumstances, if you've been hurt, go to God in prayer. Take your Bible and cover it with your tears. Allow God's Holy Spirit to lift your crushed spirit. Corrie ten Boom once said, "There is no pit so deep that God's love is not deeper still (*The Hiding Place*)."

After you've poured out your heart to God, find someone in whom you can confide.

Allow God's healing in your life. Allow him to fill every nook and cranny of your heart with his love and surrender your life to him. Choose to spend the rest of your life living in forgiveness— sometimes just one moment, then one hour, then one day, then one week, then one year, then five years, then ten years. And then a lifetime.

Focus on this moment—that's all you have. Let God worry about the tomorrows. Be set free from your unresolved anger by focusing on the process of forgiving. The outcome is in God's hands.

DEAR JESUS, I know you love me, warts and all. I have sinned against you and others. I am separated from your love

because of my sin. I know that you're the only way to eternal life.

You made salvation possible through your death on the cross. Your resurrection is proof that you're who you say you are. I accept you into my heart. Thank you, Jesus, for coming into my life right now. Thank you for forgiving me of my sins.

CHAPTER 21

PERFECT LOVE CASTS OUT FEAR

THERE IS no fear in love, but perfect love casts out fear.

—I John 4:18a

In *The Donkey and the King,* Much-Afraid, the dog, shook with fear when Baruch left her behind at the stable. During the time the donkey was gone, the king helped Much-Afraid to conquer her fear.

From *Seventh Dimension – The Door, a Young Adult Christian Fantasy.*

The dog stretched and cocked her head enjoying the rubdown.

I laughed. "Is your name Much-Afraid?"

"I was always afraid until the king healed me."

—Shale Snyder and Much-Afraid, the dog, chapter ten

When we meet Much-Afraid again in *Seventh Dimension – The Door*, she has overcome her fear.

Do you know that the opposite of fear is love? Every time you're afraid, that means you're not allowing God's love into your heart. God's perfect love will cast out your imperfect fear. In fact, your imperfect fear is made perfect in weakness. In your weakness, God can help you. Once you recognize your weakness, you won't rely on yourself and your own abilities. You will rely on God.

Begin with prayer. Most of us struggle with fear at times because we don't love perfectly. Our humanness makes us needy, but our sin keeps us from embracing God's unconditional love. In spite of this, God never gives up. He woos us because we're cherished, like a lover woos his beloved.

The king told Shale, "I love you more than you will ever know." In the same way, God loves you. Someday when we meet the king, we'll truly know how much he loves us.

Every time fear threatens you (and I do believe in demons of fear), remember the words of the king. Let his perfect love fill your mind. Let every cell within you find intimacy in your heavenly father. Don't rely on yourself. You will fall. Find your strength in God. Don't be just a fan of Jesus Christ, like on Facebook or Twitter. Be a follower. Make Jesus your king and your lord. Let his love conquer any fear that creeps into your heart. Then you will be able to love others in the same way God loves you.

Your heavenly father is waiting for you to surrender. He is never too busy to listen, and I guarantee you, he is not resting.

The king died to defeat every fear Satan will tempt you to believe. Don't be seized with a knot in your stomach and crippling doubts.

Let God's love indwell you. Cast aside every anxious thought. Don't give up. Don't give in. Don't wait. Begin by reading the Bible and then pray for God to be real to you—

more real than he has ever been in the past. His perfect love will cast out your fear.

If you do this every time you become fearful, you can claim victory. If you don't succeed the first time, don't give up, especially if you're prone to being fearful. Old habits die hard, and Satan is relentless. But God will help if you're faithful in prayer and read your Bible.

If you still struggle with fear after much prayer, perhaps you might need to see a counselor or physician. Sometimes chemical imbalances can affect your mood, especially if you're going through a particularly difficult time.

Don't be afraid or embarrassed. Ask for help. Pride will tell you, you don't need crutches, but humility is more powerful than pride.

Thank you, Jesus, for loving me. Help me to feel loved. Help me to trust you every time I feel afraid.

CHAPTER 22

GOD MEANS IT FOR GOOD

As for me, you [Joseph's brothers] meant evil against me [Joseph], but God meant it for good in order to bring about this present result, to preserve many people alive.

Genesis 50:20

I have to remind myself there is good in the world and it's worth fighting for. Especially when bad things happen or someone treats me unfairly.

※

FROM *SEVENTH DIMENSION – The Door, a Young Adult Christian Fantasy*.

Her voice trailed off as she read a few more lines to herself. Then, with one fell swoop, she threw my paper in the trash.

"This is too well written to be original. I'm sure Shale copied it off the web. I'm not going to read it."

Thirty sets of eyes shifted to me and my face and neck felt hot. Mrs. Wilkes' beady eyes pulsated. No one moved. If I dropped the straight pin that was in my sweater pocket, the room would have heard it ping on the floor.

—Mrs. Wilkes and Shale Snyder, chapter two

AM I OKAY, GOD?

❧

Have you ever felt unfairly accused of something you didn't do? Or something happened that was unfair?

How could God use what happened to Shale for good? Shale's writing ability was far beyond her years, so the teacher thought she had plagiarized her report. But Shale's insecurity kept her from seeing her true value. The teacher's accusations stung. Whatever talent she did have for writing was overshadowed by the pain she felt inside.

My favorite story in the Bible is the story of Joseph. God chose Joseph to save the nation of Israel. Before God's plan was revealed, however, Joseph's brothers sold him into slavery. The brothers were filled with jealousy toward Joseph because their father had given Joseph a beautiful coat of many colors, but he had not given one to each of them. Later, Joseph was falsely accused by someone else and sent to prison for something he didn't do.

The only thing we can control is our attitude and our response to all the things that go wrong.

We're like soldiers in a war zone fighting evil. No matter what, God is on our side. We must not allow the evil to consume us with bitterness. We don't want anything to become an idol or to come before God. The first commandment in the Bible says, "You shall have no other gods before me" (Exodus 20:3).

I find it helpful to remember that God knows the beginning and the end. He knows when I have been wronged and treated unfairly.

I will share a secret. I was accused of plagiarism by a teacher when I was in fifth grade. It never occurred to me at the time that I had a gift of writing. All I could think of was how embarrassed I was that the teacher had accused me in front of the class and I couldn't defend myself.

But what Satan intended for evil, God meant for good. Today I have an opportunity to share my experience with you and to encourage you. I can remind you that God knows the truth about your situation, just as he knew the truth about me. He knew someday I would become an author and write about these things, and use these bad experiences to bring him glory.

Can you encourage someone who may be going through a difficult situation? God will not waste opportunities. Allow him to redeem the bad and the ugly. That's the best part about being a Christian. Whatever Satan does to cause problems, God always has the final word. God knows how to make lemonade from lemons.

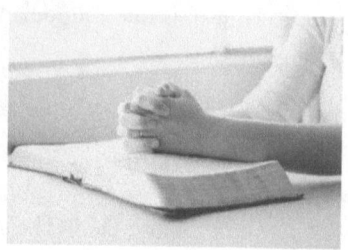

Thank you, Jesus, that you know the beginning and the end. Thank you that everything in my life you can use for good—even the bad parts. Please help me not to become discouraged but to keep my eyes on you. Help me to remember that everything that happens passes through your permissive hand. Thank you that I can trust you in all these things.

CHAPTER 23

BECOMING

. . .

I GAVE you milk to drink, not solid food; for you were not yet able to receive it. Indeed, even now you are not able to receive it.

—I Corinthians 3:2

We are born. We get married. We raise kids. We pay taxes. Then we die.

FROM *SEVENTH DIMENSION — The Door, a Young Adult Christian Fantasy* quoted from Shakespeare's play, *The Tempest*.

ALL THE WORLD'S A STAGE.

And all the men and women merely players

They have their exits and their entrances

And one man in his time plays many parts

His acts being seven ages.

—Mrs. Wilkes, chapter two

SOUNDS DEPRESSING, doesn't it? While the above statement is an exaggeration, at times I have felt like life is far too woeful with little reward. But without God, life would be a hundred times worse.

Goodness in the world is an extension of God's love. Hardship is an extension of his grace. How much darker the world would be without God's presence. Would we even know the difference between good and evil without the Holy Spirit? I am thankful for absolutes. God does not change, and when I feel threatened, I am comforted by knowing that God holds everything together.

You lose your job, your home, your health—God allows it. An accident lands you in the hospital—God allows it. Sorrow is part of the human condition—all over the world.

Hurricanes, tornadoes, earthquakes, and floods ravage and destroy property. The toll on human life is difficult to comprehend. "Why, God?"

Randomness is universal to us. God causes it to rain on the just and unjust.

I used to think I suffered because I was bad. I thought bad things happened because I deserved it. Some Christians will tell you that if you get a disease, it's because there is sin in your life or you don't have enough faith. If you had more faith, you would be healed of your disease.

Or if you suffer economic hardship, you must have done something to cause a reversal in your fortunes—something you did displeased God.

Perhaps, when I was young, this is where I got the idea that I was born under a cloud. You shouldn't make that correlation because it's not true.

Bad things happen to good people. Good things happen to bad people. Why? We live in a fallen, sinful world. Although God is in control, he allows events to happen. While life might seem random to us, it's not random to God.

Why do bad things happen? I don't know. I don't know the mind of God. I have often said, when I get to heaven, I want him to tell me why he allowed this thing to happen or that thing to happen. Then I quickly remind myself, when I see him, it will no longer matter. He will wipe away my tears.

Besides, God already knows the outcome. The process is for our benefit—to reveal what's in our heart. How much do we really love God? Do we only love him when we receive good things from him and not hard things? How well do we know ourselves?

God cares about the process. If the process of suffering draws us nearer to him, then God can be glorified in our suffering. When I feel that I can't take "it" anymore, God reminds me that my momentary afflictions will not be remembered in heaven. One of my favorite expressions is, "this, too, shall pass."

Besides that, where else can we go? If we hit rock bottom, where will we turn? Who holds the answers? Who understands us? If we can glorify God despite hardship and loss and suffering, then we know we love God—not because he gives us good things, but because we know he is with us in the hard things.

Throughout history, Christians have suffered at the hands of others. Corrie ten Boom and her sister Betsie were taken to a concentration camp during World War II after helping Jews to escape the Holocaust. Betsie died while in the camp.

Foxe's Book of Martyrs shares the testimonies of Christians who have died for their faith. I tried to read this book with my older daughter when we homeschooled. I couldn't quit crying.

An average of 159,960 Christians worldwide are martyred for their faith each year (http://christianity.about.com/od/denominations/p/christiantoday.htm).

While you may never suffer persecution, there are other forms of suffering. There's disease, hunger, disability, hardship, and death. God never promised that Christians wouldn't suffer. A student is never above his master. Jesus suffered unimaginable pain and separation from God when he died on the cross. If God wanted to spare the death of his son on the cross, surely he could have avoided the process, but he chose not to.

Jesus asked for the cup to be taken from him, but it didn't happen. Jesus willingly chose to die. Thousands of angels would have come to his rescue had he asked. He didn't. Jesus willingly died for you and for me. That was his passion, and God has given you yours.

It's in the process that we choose how we shall live—what our attitudes will be and what choices we'll make. Are we willing to sacrifice and toil and labor for the God whom we claim we love, or will we succumb to our sinful nature. Life is about the process. We're born and we die, but it's all the stuff in between about which God cares.

When you enter college, you meet with a guidance counselor who will create a plan for your four-year academic career. For example, if you want to be a doctor, you must take calculus. At the end of the semester, you must take a test to see if you have mastered the subject. You can't graduate from college if you don't pass all your tests and complete the requirements laid out for you by the counselor.

If we never faced challenges, we would never be tested. God tested Abraham when he asked Abraham to sacrifice his son, Isaac. God knew what Abraham would choose, but did Abraham himself know? The process of becoming reveals to us who we are in Christ.

In the same way, God has a plan. His plan is to help you become more like Jesus. Our sanctification, the process of becoming, will not be completed here. In *Pilgrims Progress*, Christian overcame many obstacles along the way, and as the name of the book implies, he progressed in his faith until God called him home. We are becoming Christian.

God gives us times of rest and times of work, times of war and times of peace, times of tearing down and times of building up, but in everything under the sun, we are becoming.

We need Christian leaders, peacemakers, and prayer warriors. These heroes of the faith aren't born that way—they have become that way. While God gives us gifts to become, it's up to us to use the talents he gives us. If we misuse our gifts or pride puffs us up, God may take away our gifts and give them to someone else.

In the low points of our life we feel the depth of God's love. *Oh, the Deep, Deep, Love of Jesus* Samuel Trevor Francis wrote in his well-known Christian hymn. Years earlier as a teenager he had contemplated suicide. Perhaps a better question to ask is not why I have suffered so much, but how much more would I have suffered without God's grace?

Only when we arrive home will we be made perfect in Jesus Christ. Until then, we are becoming—and suffering is part of that process—our passion.

Dear Jesus, when bad things happen, you are with me. Even if I am fearful, I will trust in you; and if I trust in you, who can separate me from your love?

CHAPTER 24

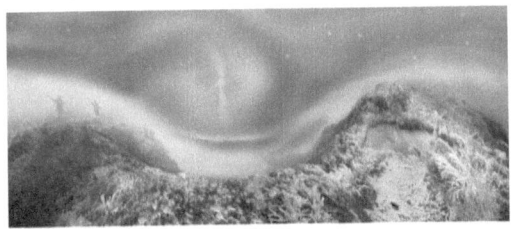

TRUTHS FROM THE OTHER SIDE

If I [Jesus] go and prepare a place for you, I will come again and receive you to myself, that where I am, there you may be also.

—John 14:3

Science fiction gives me the ability to travel to faraway places —and I like the exotic. In reality, Scotty can't beam me up, I can't travel to Mars, and I can't live under the ocean.

But what if I could walk through walls? What if I could die and come back to life? What if I could read other people's minds, talk to animals, travel through time, and visit the spiritual world through a hidden door?

From *Seventh Dimension – The Door, a Young Adult Christian Fantasy*

"Will the king always be with me?"

"Always. The seventh dimension is within you."

—Shale Snyder and Astello, chapter thirty-seven.

THE SEVENTH DIMENSION is a place beyond time. It's within you and amongst the stars, but a heartbeat away and a prayer close by in times of need. God is ever mindful of what we do and where we are. If we feel estranged, we have moved—not God.

The Bible says many unusual things happened on the night of Jesus' crucifixion, events often overlooked by the casual reader. I mention some of those strange apparitions in *The Door* to draw attention to the fact that much of what happened at the cross was supernatural. Supernatural means what it says—unnatural to the world we can see and feel and touch. I call it the seventh dimension.

Matthew 27:45 says from the sixth hour until the ninth hour, darkness came over all the land.

Matthew 27:46 says Jesus cried out in a loud voice, "My God, my God, why have you forsaken me!" He didn't cry out to one of his followers or his family. He cried out to God.

When Jesus gave up his spirit, Matthew 27:51 says the curtain of the temple was torn in two from top to bottom. The earth shook and the rocks split. Tombs broke open and dead people came out of them. After Jesus' resurrection, they went into Jerusalem and appeared to many people.

Those that saw this exclaimed, "Surely he was the son of God" (Matthew 27:54).

A violent earthquake shook the ground following Passover. An angel rolled away the stone from the tomb and sat on it. Matthew 28:3-4 says, "His appearance was like lightning, and his clothes were white as snow. The guards shook for fear of him and became like dead men."

Later that day, Jesus met the women who had followed him and his disciples. Over and over, he told his followers, "Do not be afraid."

Stop and think. Imagine you had been there. You witness two earthquakes, see something strange in the sky, hear about the tearing of the curtain in the Jewish temple, and are told dead people have come back to life. One of them even appeared to you—your uncle who died five years ago. You hear rumors of an angel appearing before the guards in the garden.

Reports spread about several appearances of Jesus, even though you saw him die on a cross. You witnessed a spear stuck in his side and nails driven into his hands and feet.

In today's world, with all of our medical technology, how long would it take someone to recover from that kind of injury, if it were even possible?

When have dead people come back to life and greeted hundreds of astonished onlookers? With the Internet, Twitter, Facebook, and around-the-clock television reporters looking for the story of the century, we would know about it immediately.

When has there been an eclipse associated with two earthquakes that occurred simultaneously?

What is the boundary between the spiritual world and the natural world? Spiritual beings can go back and forth—humans can't. Jesus' resurrection is proof that a person can come back from the dead. He was the first to be raised.

While his disciples recognized him, he appeared strangely different. They witnessed him travel through walls. He was no longer bound by the limitations of a human body. Something supernatural happened—that had never happened before.

All these things were possible because there's a seventh dimension—a reality we can't see or touch or feel—a reality that is outside of time as we know it. God's reality is bigger than we can perceive because we are mortal.

When sin entered the garden and tainted God's creation, it took away the immortality of humans. The unique relationship that man had with God in the garden ended. Death began and time took on a different meaning. Man would count the days, grow old, and die.

When Jesus died, he conquered sin once and for all. We will still suffer a physical death if the Lord tarries, but God will resurrect us so we can live with him forever in heaven. Those who have not received Jesus' salvation will also suffer a physical death, but they will be resurrected to spend an eternity in hell.

We only have glimpses into the world of angels and demons—like we can see the introduction to a movie, catch scenes of what's to come, but we can't "see" the movie until the movie hits theaters.

We have visual clues into a world beyond this one—evidence that demands our attention.

Jesus said in Luke 17:21 that the kingdom of God is within us. Because we are made in God's image, his image is imprinted on us—in our synapses and in every breath we take. We long to be known by our Creator. We are the created: loved and molded in the Creator's image.

Shale's adventure into the seventh dimension is what happens to all of us at some level once we begin our quest for truth—a truth that is unlimited. The spirit from beyond teaches us about things we can't understand naturally. Science has no answers for spiritual truths. They must be perceived spiritually.

When we die, we leave earth and go somewhere. We don't stay here. No human has ever escaped the inevitable except two men in the Old Testament. In both cases, their being "taken up" without death was to glorify God.

Martyrs throughout history have also glorified God in their deaths—a testimony to everyone who comes after them. We are but a vapor, here today and gone tomorrow, but we hold the truth within us. God wants us to share that truth with a world that needs more love—God's love.

In the last book of the Bible, we are given a detailed account of the seventh dimension. John, the disciple whom Jesus loved, was imprisoned on the island of Patmos. He was an old man as this vision happened many years after the crucifixion. John was told by an angel to write down everything he saw.

John was given a glimpse into the future. He saw many events yet to take place, mysteries, terrifying images for which he had no words. His writings make up what is known as the Revelation.

... AND THE LIVING ONE; and I [Jesus] was dead, and behold, I am alive forevermore, and I have the keys of death and Hades.

—Revelation 1:18

I CAN'T DO justice to understanding Revelation, but I have thought about what certain things mean many times—the receding of the scroll, how John could see so far into the future, why God gave him the vision, and what God wants us to learn. Revelation is the only book in the Bible that offers a blessing to those who read it.

BLESSED IS he who reads and those who hear the words of the prophecy, and heed the things which are written in it; for the time is near.

—Revelation 1:3

IMAGINE there is a ruler timeline for the whole universe. You're a tiny, insignificant dot in the year 20__. You can see only a sliver of what's on that timeline. That's your reality. But the seventh dimension covers the whole timeline and keeps on going past the edge of the ruler forwards and backwards. A ruler is only two dimensions—but the seventh dimension is, well, who knows how many dimensions? I chose seven because it's the most sacred number in the Bible.

Let's take another example. You're a fish in an aquarium. That is your world, perhaps located in the corner of the living room. When you look through the glass of the aquarium, you see a world that you don't understand. People outside the tank seem like gods to you. They dump flakes of fish food in your tank—they keep you alive.

LORILYN ROBERTS

Your three-dimensional world is only as big as the fish tank. Because you don't understand the outside world doesn't mean it doesn't exist. You see distorted glimpses of it through the aquarium glass.

For now we see in a mirror dimly, but then face-to-face; now I know in part, but then I will know fully just as I also have been fully known.

— *I Corinthians 13:12*

Shale was known by Jesus long before she knew who he was. She sensed there was something she wanted, but she didn't know what it was. She longed for something she could not name. Have you ever felt that way?

That longing is for Jesus Christ. Jesus was fully human and fully God. He died and was resurrected on the third day. He now assumes his godly position in heaven. The Messianic Jews accept Jesus for who he said he was. They call him their Messiah. The king resides in heaven now, his abode.

In *Seventh Dimension – The Door*, the bird cage descended from heaven and alighted on the king's out-spread palm. Then he opened the door of the cage and set the small bird free.

The symbolism is powerful. In the same way the king set the bird free, Jesus freed Shale. You are that beautiful bird in a cage waiting—to be freed from sin, freed from impediments that blind you and bind you. You're as free as you give yourself permission to be—free to become all God created you to be.

Don't place limitations on yourself—your lack of belief, your lack of trust, your lack of faith—your lack in these areas is because of sin. Sin limits your ability to receive love. Jesus came to set you free. That freedom is yours once you commit your life to him.

Your freedom is a gift—Jesus Christ will not force himself on you. He is a gentleman in every sense of the word—a perfect gentleman. You must choose to let him into your heart.

IF YOU ABIDE IN ME, and my words abide in you, ask whatever you wish, and it will be done for you.

—John 15:7

YOU HAVE BEEN GIVEN everything you need to live a godly life in the person of Jesus Christ. Take a moment and ponder where you want to spend eternity. Remember, you're no more than a worm, but Christ was willing to become as lowly as a worm in order to save you.

Out of the seventh dimension greatness visited us in the form of a king. He left his throne and entered the abode of man. He became one of us so we could become one of his.

In our flesh, limited by our ability to see the supernatural, we see God through general creation. But we must open our eyes to see. We must not let depravity steal our joy. We must not let evilness wax our love cold. The choice to heed God's calling is ours.

Dear Jesus, I have sinned against you and others. You died for me on the cross, my only way to heaven. Please come into my heart and help me to follow you. Thank you for your gift of salvation.

CHAPTER 25

THE NEW HEAVEN AND EARTH

AND I HEARD a loud voice from the throne, saying, "Behold, the tabernacle of God is among men, and he will dwell among them, and they shall be his people, and God himself will be among them, and he will wipe away every tear from their eyes; and there will no longer be any death; there will no longer be any mourning, or crying, or pain; the first things have passed away.

—*Revelation 21:3-5*

Would you like to visit the garden in *Seventh Dimension – The Door*? Evil lurked in that garden, but when Jesus returns, he will create a new earth free of sin.

FROM *SEVENTH DIMENSION – The Door, a Young Adult Christian Fantasy.*

Evening came. I wanted to love but I was unwilling to give up my hate. Could the king's words penetrate my hardened heart? What joy would fill me if I surrendered everything to the king?

Baruch nudged me with his nose. "Where do we go now, Miss Shale?"

The crowds were leaving to return to their homes. I didn't feel like I had one. I closed my eyes and prayed. "If I'm a daughter of the king, please forgive me. I'm sorry for my wrong attitude."

Nothing changed on the outside, but I felt better on the inside."

—Shale Snyder, chapter thirty-two

WHILE I CAN'T CHANGE the world I face each day, I can cleanse my thoughts through reading the Bible. I can pray when I am driving, when I am cooking, or when I rise or go to bed. I can confess to God my pain when I feel overwhelmed by the unexplained darkness—when bad things happen.

By allowing God to work in my heart, I can gain a heavenly perspective, lifting my spirit from the gutter that robs me of my joy.

Take a few moments and imagine what God is preparing for you. Your negative thoughts can be redeemed, helping you to live each day with renewed hope for a brighter future.

Someday, God's new heaven and new earth will rise from the ashes following the greatest war ever fought in the universe. God and his angelic warriors will fight in the last battle against Satan and the demons of darkness. Earth will be the battleground and man the prized possession.

While man's salvation is already secured by Jesus' death and resurrection, the finality of souls' destination is only within God's purview. Satan does not know; neither does he know everything you think. Satan is not omniscient. He has nothing to lose—except you.

Even as the battle wages, once we accept Jesus, we can rejoice. We can know for certain where we will live for eternity.

Where is heaven? A place where our failures will no longer paralyze us; where perfect love casts out fear, pure joy abounds with unceasing laughter, and unfettered peace will last forever. It's but one heartbeat away for those who believe in Jesus Christ.

Until we enter heaven's gates, we have to deal with sin. The curse, passed down from Adam and Eve, plagues all creatures. Everything eventually dies.

The best thing about heaven is Jesus lives there—as king. No more elections, no more dictators, and no more czars. He said he was going to prepare a place for his followers, and someday he would return and take us back with him.

What will we see, and what will we look like?

Heaven is inhabited by millions of beautiful angelic creatures. When we pass through heaven's gates, we will be clothed in spiritual bodies that will no longer be physically imperfect but eternally perfect.

Some saints will shine brighter than others, depending on their faithfulness to God, just as some stars appear brighter in the night sky. There will be rewards for our good works and for bringing others into the kingdom.

In heaven, there's no competition for food or toll for survival—even in the animal kingdom.

. . .

FOR WE KNOW that the whole creation groans and suffers the pains of childbirth together until now.

—Romans 8:22

THE WOLF and the lamb will feed beside each other. Children will play with lions. The sound of crying will never be heard again. The old order of things will have passed away. When God wipes away our tears, our afflictions and troubles will no longer be remembered.

Heaven is never dark because the glory of God gives it light. The New Jerusalem will radiate with the majesty of God. The city will be built of gold, pure as glass. The foundations of the walls will glitter with precious gems and the twelve gates made of pearl will greet city visitors. Nothing impure will ever enter the city.

The River of Life will flow from God's throne, and the Tree of Life in the city square will bear a different fruit each month. Its leaves will be for the healing of nations. Whatever we have here will be even better there—in beauty, fullness, and purity.

Heaven in Revelation has many mysteries beyond our understanding. The four winds who obey God and the four creatures who give praise to our heavenly father—who are they?

The Bible doesn't give us a map to heaven, but in Genesis 28:12, Jacob "had a dream, and …a ladder was set on the earth with its top reaching to heaven; and … the angels of God were ascending and descending on it."

In Revelation 4:1, John saw an open door to heaven; and in Acts 7:56, Stephen said, "I see heaven open and the Son of Man standing at the right hand of God."

Because it's impossible for anything defiled or sinful to enter through the gates, it would have been impossible for anyone to go there if God had not provided a way. God said in Leviticus 26:12, "I will walk among you and be your God, and you will be my people."

Today we battle against the unseen powers of darkness—the prince of the air and his demonic minions. But through the Holy Spirit, we have a taste of heaven here. When we receive Jesus into our hearts, the Comforter indwells us. The Spirit whispers to us in our sleep, comforts us in our pain, and implores us never to give up.

The Bible reminds us of God's unwavering truth. Thousands of years of attacks upon it and God's chosen have strengthened the validity of the Bible's claims. Even the rocks would cry out in praise to the heavenly father if it were possible.

When Jesus hung on the cross, he said to one of the two thieves beside him, "Truly, today you will be with me in paradise" (Luke 23:43). I take comfort in the fact that for the last two thousand years, Jesus has been preparing a place for you and for me.

Someday heavenly music will fill our ears. We will splash with joy in heavenly waters emanating from God's throne and walk on streets of gold. We will be reunited with those who have gone before us. We will feast at the marriage supper of the Lamb, and all those whose names are written in the Book of Life will see the face of God.

. . .

In this world you will have trouble. But take heart! I have overcome the world.

— John 16:33

WHAT A GLORIOUS ETERNITY AWAITS US. Until that day, let not the heartaches of this world discourage us from remembering the richness of God's grace here—found in Jesus Christ.

I am thankful I am a daughter (or son) of the king. I am thankful that my salvation is assured through Jesus' death and resurrection. Help me to honor the king in all my ways so that he may be glorified— until I enter the pearl gates of heaven.

CHAPTER 26

WHAT NOW?

...*AND LO, I [Jesus] am with you always, even to the end of the age.*

—*Matthew 28:20*

When I was ten, I had a dream. In the dream I was listening to a song by Johnny Mathis on my record player. Over the music, I heard a voice that sounded like rushing waters that echoed from far away. The voice said, "Today is judgment day." Frightened, I woke up from the dream with my heart pounding. Was it really judgment day?

From *Seventh Dimension – The Door, a Young Adult Christian Fantasy.*

"War, famine, pestilence, financial collapse. America suffers the most—their military decimated by spending cuts. The dollar collapses because of the mounting debt and Washington's unwillingness or inability to cut frivolous spending. China takes over as the dominant world power and Islam seizes control of many governments. The world is aflame."

—Daniel, chapter fourteen

AM I OKAY, GOD?

AFTER THAT DREAM, I asked, what happens when you die? When is the end of the world? Is there a judgment day? Would I be judged?

I asked my father and he said, "Yes, there's a judgment day and everybody will be judged." He suggested I listen to Billy Graham on the radio.

Not long after that, I watched Billy Graham on TV speaking at one of his international crusades. In those days, the crusades were carried live.

Billy Graham was the consummate evangelist. His sermons were always about judgment, salvation, and the end times. He never sugarcoated anything. I later bought some of his books and often read his column in the newspaper. I was blessed to attend two of his crusades in person—including the last one he ever spoke at in Jacksonville, Florida.

For years, when Dr. Graham gave the altar call, I recited the sinner's prayer to receive salvation—in case I didn't do it right the previous time. Who knows how many times I said that prayer until I realized I didn't need to keep saying it. Jesus already lived in my heart. But I struggled, thinking I could lose my salvation. I compare that experience to worrying about the unpardonable sin. If you worry about committing the unpardonable sin, chances are good you don't have anything to worry about.

I received the gift of salvation when I read the Gospel of Matthew at twelve. My spirit was moved by one thing—Jesus' love for the oppressed people and his compassion on those who were hurting.

I was also fascinated by the "proof texts" found in Matthew.

Because of my familiarity with Jewish things and having briefly attended a Sunday school class that studied the Old Testament, I'd learned a lot about Moses and the prophets. I knew that the Old Testament predicted a Messiah would come and bring salvation to the Jewish people. Matthew cites some of those predictions found in Isaiah, Micah, Hosea, and Daniel.

When I read Matthew, I became convinced that Jesus was the Messiah. The "proof texts" were overwhelmingly accurate, predictions made and recorded in Jewish literature hundreds of years earlier.

I will never forget reading Matthew 24:1 – 25:46 for the first time. The disciples asked Jesus, "When will these things happen, and what will be the sign of your coming?"

I had the same question as the disciples. Could Jesus return during my lifetime? Would we be able to recognize the signs of his return?

In my teens I read the book *666* by Salem Kirban. A few years later I read *The Late Great Planet Earth* by Hal Lindsey. Probably these two books, both of which were inspired by the book of Revelation, influenced me spiritually more than any other books as a teenager besides the Bible.

During my freshman year at the University of Georgia, Hal Lindsey came to the university and spoke. I was intrigued and wanted to learn more, but the seed that had been planted stayed dormant for a long time.

While many years have passed since I read Revelation for the first time, I have never forgotten some of my early thoughts about the book. When it described an army of 200 million men in Revelation 9:16, most scholars agreed the only country in the world that could outfit that many soldiers would be China. I laughed. Back in those days, China was a third-world nation. There was no way they could become a world power and form an army like that. Or could they?

Revelation 20:4 says, "Then I saw thrones, and they sat on them, and judgment was given to them. And I saw the souls of those who had been beheaded because of their testimony of Jesus and because of the word of God, and those who had not worshipped the beast or his image and had not received the mark on their forehead and on their hand; and they came to life and reigned with Christ for a thousand years."

What group of people or country or religious sect in today's civilized world beheads Christians? I considered that barbaric when I was a teen. Surely that couldn't be right—or could it?

World events are hurtling forward at an increasingly rapid pace. Events that were hard to imagine even a few years ago are accepted—even promoted. Until recently, most people would have doubted that society would accept as normal the marrying of two men or two woman.

Some people believe that the cultural and moral changes in the U.S. today will lead directly to the violence portrayed in Revelation. It's not hard to imagine how events as predicted in Revelation could happen in the next few years leading to Armageddon.

I wait expectantly for the rebuilding of the Jewish Temple, one piece of the puzzle that seems to be needed before all of the events as foretold by Jesus can happen. How else could there be the "abomination of desolation" as spoken of in Matthew 24:15?

My intent here is not to go into a detailed dissertation about the end times and prophecy, but to pique your interest to pursue your own study. Where might you be in ten years, twenty years, or thirty years? If the United States continues on its current path, will we even exist as a free country?

While most of your day is probably consumed with more relevant and pressing issues; i.e., peer pressure, money, what you're going to study in college, or when the next *Star Trek* movie will be at the theater (I am a Trekkie too), your generation faces great challenges. It's important to ask, what now? What are my priorities? What about my future?

Make a list of what's most important to you. Otherwise, the tyranny of the urgent will suck out of you every ounce of energy, time, and money you possess, leaving you spiritually dry.

Make God a priority. Find time to pray and read your Bible. Get involved in a local church. Christianity is not so much a religion as a relationship—a relationship with God and other Christians.

God never intended for Christians to be loners. My prayer group that meets on Wednesday nights helps me to get through the week. I feel encouraged when I leave, knowing that I have prayed for others and others have prayed for me. I have been in a prayer group for the last twenty-seven years. The people with whom I've prayed I've regarded at different times to be my closest friends. Some have moved away. Some have died. Some are in other groups now. But when you pray with someone, you share your soul. You share what's most important.

Remember: The relationships you form here will continue in heaven. I remember answers to prayers from twenty years ago. I may not recall the name of a person I met an hour ago, but if someone asks me to pray for him or her, I will remember it.

The Holy Spirit intercedes and remembers every prayer ever prayed and brings to mind those requests. I believe that when we pray here, we truly make a difference in the spiritual realm. We tear down evil strongholds. We send the demons scampering because they can't bear to hear Jesus' name.

What now? Trust and obey God, surrendering your will to his. Know the end is near. Jesus' return could happen tomorrow. Live your life to the fullest. Make the most of every opportunity because the days are evil.

Watch the news and be informed. Christians need to be aware of what is happening in the world. Perhaps if Christians hadn't buried their heads in the sand when Hitler came to power, the church could have prevented the slaughter of six million Jews.

The future world leader promising peace will be worse than Hitler or Stalin. This anti-Christ will deceive many. Be alert. While your salvation is assured, God needs you to his hands and feet and mind and soul—to carry out the Great Commission.

Don't lose heart. And don't lose sleep over the future. I like to imagine John saw me 2,000 years ago in his vision— fighting the good fight, defending the Gospel, standing for the truth, and even being a martyr if that's what I'm called to be.

Jesus says at the end of the book of Revelation, "I am coming soon" (Revelation 22:7). Are you ready?

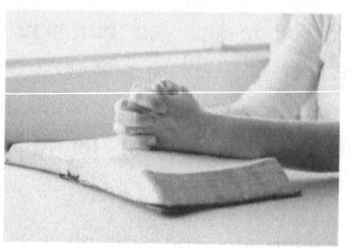

Yes! Come quickly, Lord Jesus.

EPILOGUE

FOR GOD SO LOVED THE WORLD, THAT HE GAVE HIS ONLY begotten Son, that whoever believes in him shall not perish, but have eternal life.

—*John 3:16*

John Piper wrote a book titled *Don't Waste Your Life*. It's one of my favorites and I would encourage you to read it. But I want to take it a step further. Think about these things:

From *Seventh Dimension – The Door, a Young Adult Christian Fantasy*

"People journey to the seventh dimension when something happens that creates a longing—so great that nothing else can fill it, except the king himself."

—Astello, chapter thirty-seven.

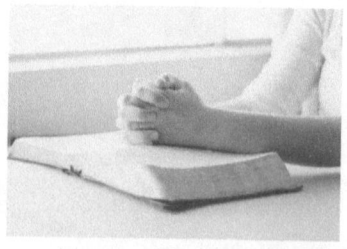

Admonish Yourself

Don't waste your life—work hard, train like an Olympian—and find your purpose in Jesus Christ.

Don't waste your education—enrich your mind with the knowledge of God's creation.

Don't waste your talents—glorify God with your creativity—make kids laugh, dancers dance, and praise God, the Creator.

Don't waste your health—you only get one body, one mind, and one spirit.

Don't waste your time—you can only spend your time once. Spend it on activities that will draw you near to God.

Don't waste your opportunity to do great things—Jesus died for you. Give him your best. He gave you his life.

Don't waste your money—many in the world need food and medicine. World Vision, Wycliffe, and Samaritan's Purse are among my favorite charities.

Don't waste your love—the world never has enough. Love until you grow weary and go to bed exhausted. The Holy Spirit will renew your strength and passion. Your tank will never run dry.

Don't waste your mind—it's too precious. Think about whatever is beautiful, whatever is noble, whatever is right, whatever is pure, and whatever is lovely. Renew your mind with the daily reading of God's word. God's Hall of Fame is filled with martyrs who died so you could own a Bible.

Don't waste this moment—if you haven't done it, accept Jesus into your heart. Once you receive his salvation, you will be filled with the Holy Spirit. He will help you to live a godly life. You may not have tomorrow. Yesterday is gone. Seize this moment—this nanosecond, and make a decision to follow Christ.

Once you have committed your life to Jesus, visit some churches and find one that meets your spiritual needs. You can also do a Google search to locate some places of worship near you.

Jesus is coming back again. He wants to receive you into his kingdom. An inheritance awaits you. In heaven, moths don't eat your dreams, burglars don't steal your wealth, and diseases don't rob you of life.

Don't waste your salvation—bring others into the kingdom. Be a witness so that others can hear the truth. Remember, eternity lasts a very, very, very long time.

ABOUT THE AUTHOR

Lorilyn Roberts is the author of fourteen books, including the award-winning *YA Seventh Dimension Series* and memoirs *Children of Dreams* and *Tails and Purrs for the Heart and Soul.* After scuba diving around the world and earning her college degree studying abroad, she settled into single motherhood, adopting two daughters from Nepal and Vietnam. She later earned a Master of Arts in Creative

Writing and is president of the Gainesville, Florida, Chapter of Word Weavers International. Lorilyn has rescued many orphaned dogs and cats, and when she isn't writing books, she provides broadcast captioning for television. In her spare time, Lorilyn is a ham radio operator and CW/Morse Code enthusiast. KO4LBS.

ALSO BY LORILYN ROBERTS

LorilynRoberts.com

Children of Dreams

As an Audiobook

Tails and Purrs for the Heart and Soul

As an Audiobook

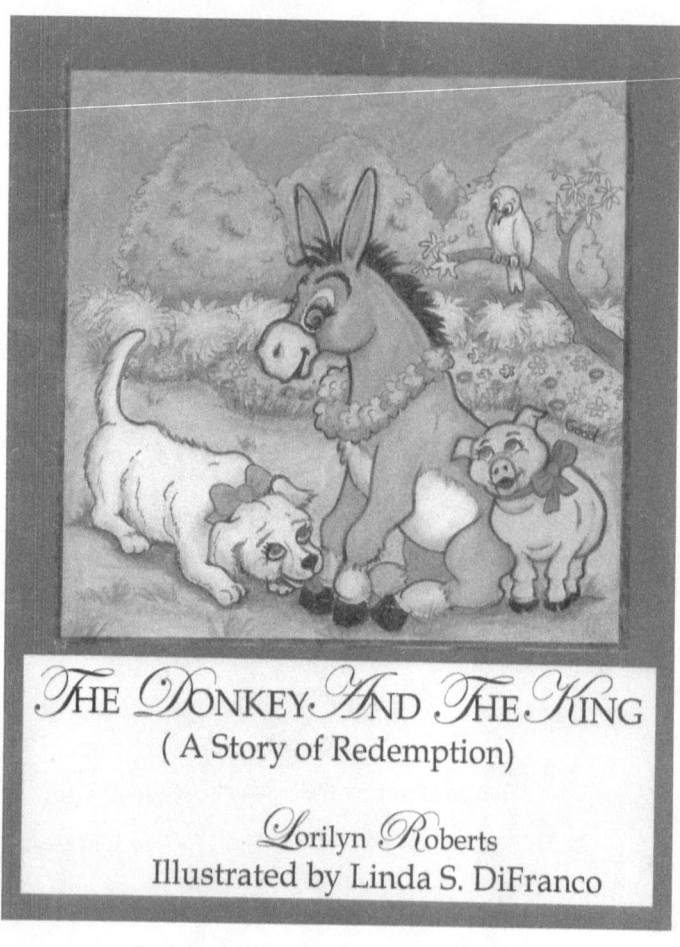

The Donkey And The King
(A Story of Redemption)

Lorilyn Roberts
Illustrated by Linda S. DiFranco

Look for the hidden word "good" on every page.

The Donkey and the King: A Story of Redemption

Young readers become world leaders.

"Book Love is beautiful inside and out."

—Joy Hannabass, Readers' Favorite Reviewer

SEVENTH DIMENSION SERIES

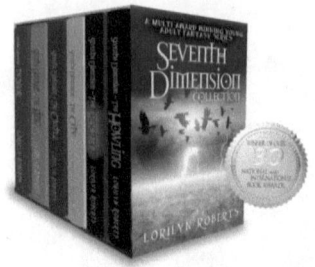

LorilynRoberts.com

Seventh Dimension - The Door, Book 1

As an Audiobook

Seventh Dimension - The King, Book 2

As an Audiobook

Seventh Dimension - The Castle, Book 3

As an Audiobook

Seventh Dimension - The City, Book 4

As an Audiobook

Seventh Dimension - The Prescience, Book 5

As an Audiobook

Seventh Dimension - The Howling, Book 6

As an Audiobook

Food For Thought: Quick and Easy Recipes for
Homeschooling Families

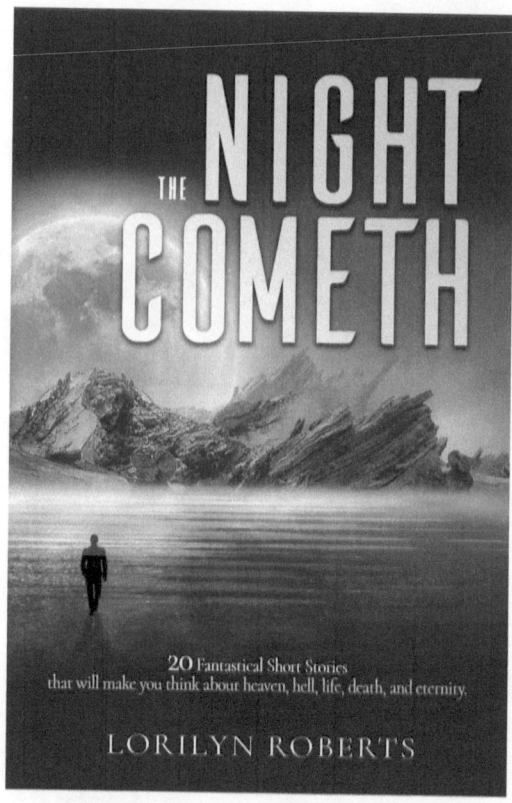

The Night Cometh: 20 Fantastical Short Stories

…that will make you think about heaven, hell, life, death, and eternity. The unsealing has begun.

- *Death stalks a man looking for answers*
- *A survivalist endures the tribulation*
- *Buckle up for a trip to hell*
- *Judgment in the court of heaven*

- *A man unwittingly sells his soul to the devil*
- *The New World Order takes over the world*
- *The United States eleven years into the future*

www.ingramcontent.com/pod-product-compliance
Lightning Source LLC
Chambersburg PA
CBHW021127300426
44113CB00006B/323